GETTING INTO

Self-
employment

JOANNA GRIGG

TROTMAN

Getting into Self-employment
This first edition published in 1999
by Trotman and Company Ltd
2 The Green, Richmond, Surrey TW9 1PL

© Joanna Grigg 1999
The right of Joanna Grigg to be identified as Author of this work has been
asserted by her in accordance with the Copyright, Design and Patent Act 1988.

British Library Cataloguing in Publication Data
A catalogue record for this book is available from the
British Library.

ISBN 0 85660 463 1

Printed and bound in Great Britain
by Creative Print & Design (Wales) Ltd

CONTENTS

INTRODUCTION

How can 28,000 people, between them:

- create 39,000 jobs?
- generate millions of pounds of business?
- save the country the cost of state benefits?

The answer: by setting up 24,000 businesses.

These people are the tip of an entrepreneurial iceberg: they are the 28,000 young people who have been helped in their new businesses by the Prince's Youth Business Trust, one of the agencies set up to keep the UK's economy healthy – and to enable us be successful if we want to become self-employed. Millions more become self-employed with help from other agencies – or even with no help at all.

Looking at self-employment from this angle – the effect it has on 'UK Ltd', may sound irrelevant right now – entrepreneurs (that's you) are generally more focused on their own personal futures and business ideas than on the national balance of payments. At this stage, perhaps:

- you simply want to sift a few ideas;
- you need answers to specific questions;
- the concept of being your own boss appeals, but you need inspiration;
- self-employment is, to you, simply a different work structure, but essentially the same as any other form of work;
- self-employment is the first step towards the conquering the world (economically, of course).

All these angles are valid, as are the many in between. This book looks at self-employment from these different viewpoints, hoping to both answer and inspire. It also aims to:

- slow you down, as rushing into business is one of the surest ways of messing it up;

- help you get your feet more firmly on the ground before you commit yourself;
- put you off, because there's a great deal more to it than many people think, and some of it might not be what you expect.

But many people who become self-employed love it:

> *'I enjoy it very much. I like meeting other people, and seeing my efforts growing. It's a very dark tunnel when you start, but once you can see the light you can see your idea happening. It might not be exactly as you thought it would be, you might need to change things, but it's nice to see it all coming together, and to see that something you're doing yourself is working.'* James Baxter, 'Arrive In Style' chauffeur service

WATCHING PEOPLE

A great way to find out what it's like to be self-employed is to watch and talk with people at the various stages of thinking about, and 'doing', self-employment. What they say won't necessarily be right for you, but will help you build a complete picture. This book contains quotes from some of these people, and from an experienced small-business adviser. Here's an introduction to the people interviewed:

Ruth

Ruth Marshall is a fine arts graduate and clothing inventor, mixing art and fashion together: 'I want to bring a bit of fantasy into our mundane lives. The sort of clothes I make are ordinary clothes that you can wear, with different features on them. A conjunction of fantasy and reality.' Ruth has a workshop and makes, wears and photographs her clothes but hasn't yet set up in business. She also works as a part-time waitress in a restaurant.

Jim

Jim McNiven set up and runs a web design agency called Kerb, and now employs three other people. He started Kerb while he was still at university. They all work long hours, in this unpredictable industry where plenty of others have already gone bust: 'We try to operate more like a gang than a company. It's a real juggling act, but it's going good.'

Matt

Matt Weyland is the Managing Director of Pulp Publications Ltd, which he set up with his wife a year ago. First, he went to a specialist college and then worked in the publishing industry for a number of years. 'We're a very new company and expanding quickly. We've spread what we print at a low level internationally, we know we'll get paid on those. These books sell throughout the year – they're not seasonal sales.'

Emma

Emma Spree set up the Learning Station Playschool six months ago. 'Two years ago my partner and I opened up our barbershop. We took that plunge and the gamble paid off, and it's doing well. When I was 5 I said "I'm going to look after babies". I've always known I would. Now I am.'

James

James Baxter set up the Arrive In Style chauffeur service with Gordon Murrell three months ago. 'We own a Bentley and the rest are all owner-drivers who we act as an agency for. We bought the car three years ago and had the whole body resprayed. The idea was to provide a car for weddings, corporate entertainment and the tourist and film industries too. We will be trading as a partnership once we have sorted a few problems out.'

Christos and Anna

Christos and Anna Stylianou are a brother and sister team who set up in business with a fashion label just over a year ago. Anna is a fashion graduate, and worked freelance for a year after graduating. Christos did a Business HND then degree, and went straight into the business: 'I do the business side, and Anna does the designing, but I've always been crazy about clothes.'

Tim

Tim Roycroft worked for a bank for many years, and then later as a small-business adviser through the enterprise agency network. 'We talk to people in business or thinking of starting in business. I am normally trying to structure their ideas into some form of business plan. A lot of people come in who aren't after finance and just need to talk through some things – we still put these in the context of a business plan.'

Throughout this book there are also quotes from students at college and university.

Some definitions

Before you use this book, note what these terms mean:

The workplace
This is the whole world of work, not one specific work location.

Self-employment
This covers anyone who works for themselves, either by setting up their own business, whether as a company or as a sole trader or partner, or working freelance. It effectively means paid work, but not working as someone's employee.

Work models or patterns
Mean structures for work, such as the model of self-employment, or the pattern of portfolio working. These are explained later in the book.

Chapter 1
IN GENERAL

WHAT IS SELF-EMPLOYMENT?

*'In business you've got to make your own money – in a bad week you
don't make any money. It's not like having a job when you get paid
anyway.'* Christos

*'The cool thing is the image we've got in the industry: every day I get
letters asking for work experience. I don't have to toe the line: I can
send out a letter if someone is pissing me off. I can totally do that if I
want – I like the freedom to mould the whole company round your
personality.'* Jim

If you are, or want to be –

- self-employed
- in business
- freelance
- working for yourself

– then you are the subject of this book. These all mean roughly the same
thing, which is that you do not have a boss who pays you a wage or salary
each week or month. Instead you:

- have an idea for providing a service or making a product;
- set this idea up as a working business, selling the service/product;
- take the income from your business;
- pay out for any overheads such as materials or rent, and things like tax
  and rates;
- keep what remains as your pay, or profit, and are liable personally for
  any shortfall (unless you form a limited company – but that is usually
  later on).

If you are 'freelance' you might not think of yourself as being 'in
business', which implies having a company and employees and providing

something visible, like constructing a building. Yet they are similar ideas when you strip them back to the basics outlined above: the person who runs the 'freelance business' or 'construction business' still takes the customer's cash and manages it, keeping any remaining profit as his or her own wages.

Different sorts of self-employment

Being self-employed means working for yourself – not having a boss telling you what to do, but making those decisions yourself. Here is a sprinkling of other terms used to describe the way people work. If you don't know them, look them up in Chapter 5: *freelance; contractor; part-timer; company director; sole trader; partner; entrepreneur*.

BUT WORK MEANS JOBS…?

We tend to talk in terms of jobs – Have you got a job? What sort of job are you looking for? and so on. It was not always like this. In fact, in most of the world it still isn't. What we really mean is: 'Have you got work?' or 'Do you have paid work?'

The Industrial Revolution changed our ideas of what work meant. Before then, work was everything we did, whether in the home or outside, whether for ourselves or somebody employing us. We would tend our patch of land as well as have several lines of expertise – both paid and unpaid work. After the Industrial Revolution we began to see work as the job we did in the city, specifically in the factory – it was work that one employer gave us. Work became jobs.

We are now going into the next stage of work – the Information Revolution. There simply aren't as many jobs any more, because organisations don't need people to be wholly theirs for long periods. Instead, they need a few 'core workers', and many more who will work on a contract basis as necessary. There is still work, but there are fewer jobs. Some experts think that the number of jobs will continue to decline, others feel that it is now steadying off. Whatever happens, it's true to say that if we look ahead at a lifetime of work only in terms of 'jobs' we may get a nasty shock. If our thinking is more flexible, we are more likely to fit into the profile of a good 'worker' rather than a disgruntled 'employee', and work is more likely to be available to us. Many commentators think that almost all this 'work' will be self-employment.

We are simply reverting to how things were, and to how they remain in many parts of the world and in some parts of our own communities. Yet it is different to what previous generations were brought up to expect, and so people tend to be wary of it. Like most things, if you understand it and adapt to it, it's not so scary. In fact, it can be very exciting.

WHO WOULD WANT TO DO IT? AND WHY?

Here are the views of some 16 and 17 year olds:

> *'I don't want to go into my own business, it's only big companies that succeed, I'd rather not put in the time and energy.'*

> *'You can do it when you want to do it. It's a good living, and better than working for someone else.'*

> *'No, I wouldn't want to. My father was self-employed and I wouldn't want to go the same way as him. He started his own company, he doesn't come home until late, he works a huge amount, he gets extremely stressed and he's been sick because of it and I don't want to end up the same way. I want to have a more relaxed life.'* You think employment is more relaxed? *'Maybe not, but at least you don't have to worry about everything yourself.'*

> *'That's the whole point about being self-employed, you don't have anyone looking down on you, you wouldn't have any constraints, but also at the same time you've got nothing to fall back on, if you work for a company they support each other whereas if you go bankrupt, who's going to look after you then?'*

Reasons for becoming self-employed; reasons for getting a job

The people above are all students at further education college: they have strong views about the prospects of working for themselves. When thinking about our own careers we often base our views on the people around us who have enjoyed self-employment, or those who have not; even those who have failed. What else can we base it on, as we don't have the experience to know otherwise? It is relatively simple, at the beginning of our working lives to look ahead at the complete package of a job that will:

- pay us regularly, and a set amount;
- train us;
- provide colleagues;
- give a safety back-up for illness;
- pay our holidays... and so on.

Most people go along this route and get a first job, even if they feel that they will eventually run their own businesses. There are plenty of good reasons for starting off in a job. These include:

- gaining experience;
- gaining skills;
- learning about the world of work;
- seeking business openings;
- making contacts;
- saving capital to start up later.

People who start this way and later go into self-employment have the best of both worlds – a knowledge of the ways and needs of organisations, and a growing certainty that they could do better, and enjoy it more, alone. Some new entrepreneurs speak positively about being self-employed:

> *'I love making my own decisions.'*
> *'I know how to do it, better than anyone else.'*
> *'I know that if I succeed, it's all down to me.'*
> *'I can't blame anyone.'*
> *'I like problem-solving, which is what it's all about.'*
> *'I'm an ideas-man and no one took my ideas seriously.'*

People also say:

> *'I make the decisions but the bank vetoes them.'*

'I made more money working in a company.'
'I work all the time – I never stop.'
'It's not like I imagined it – good, but not as good.'
'I haven't had a holiday since I set up the business.'
'I get lots of slack time.'
'I can't afford to be ill – and that makes me ill.'
'Failure is always just around the corner.'

Many small businesses do fail. But many succeed, grow, employ people and even export goods and services. Many people make an adequate living from self-employment, and some go on to become wealthy. One successful entrepreneur views his work and achievements like this:

> *'I've tried to fail as much as possible because the one thing I noticed about all successful people is that they all fail a lot. Really it's only by failing that you're going to succeed. You have to follow your fear to follow your destiny. When I feel uncomfortable I know that I am in the right place. To be scared is a very healthy place to be because it means that you're doing something.'* Simon Woodruffe, founder of Yo! Sushi chain of restaurants (from the *Independent on Sunday* 15 November 1998)

A few people never get jobs: they go straight into some form of self-employment, and stay there. This is more likely if your family and friends work this way, as you will be used to the concept, and may have their practical and emotional backing. Although jobs give many people the start they need, there are other ways:

> *'If you've got a business degree you know all there is to know about running a business. While at college I ran a young enterprise company, so I got to know how to run a business.'* Christos

So, people have different routes in, and different reasons for becoming self-employed:

- they have no choice;
- they want to become rich;
- they want a challenge;
- it is the obvious thing to do;

- they want to feel the fear;
- they want autonomy;
- they want to prove they can do it;

and plenty more reasons, too.

It is said that entrepreneurs have a certain skill: the right attitude. If you feel that starting your own business is exciting, and that the journey into the unknown is something positive, it is likely that you have the 'gene' for it. If it terrifies you, it is possible that you are not yet ready. But remember what Simon Woodruffe says – there is always fear. The unknown is scary and we have the choice – we can go out there and explore it, or settle for something a little closer to home, something more familiar. Either is valid, and both are revisable throughout our working lives. What we must ensure is that we use our learning and working time gaining what we need for the world of work, and specifically for keeping open the possible option of becoming self-employed. This means gaining the right education and the right skills. The next two chapters of this book explore these: Chapter 2 on education; Chapter 3 on experience and gaining skills.

DIFFERENT WAYS TO WORK

This is a summary of the usual patterns that we work to. Some are more common than others. If you want to find out about full-time permanent employment, you will easily find somebody to chat to. If you are looking for a portfolio worker you might have to hunt a bit longer. Talking to people about their working patterns is a helpful start in deciding what you want: they may love what they do and how they do it; you, in turn, may feel similarly, or believe you would feel the opposite. Both extremes are useful indications of what you might enjoy.

Full-time employment

This is still the normal work pattern. It generally means working for one employer for a 37–40 hour week, either the standard 9–5, or in a shift pattern to suit the employer's, or employee's, needs. Many full-time workers do in fact work far more than this every week, either because they need the overtime payments or because it's expected of them, and they can't say no. Sometimes extra hours are routinely paid; in other, higher level work, you would not expect remuneration for the extra input.

Part-time employment

This is becoming more common as the workplace changes. Up to a third of all jobs could be part-time by 2010. It can mean working just a few hours a week, or up to about 30, at which point people start thinking of you as full-time. There are many variations: you might work a job-share, where you share a full-time job, usually with one other person. You might work term-time only, to fit in with the family, or evenings only, for example to fit in with the needs of the hospitality industry.

Although part-time work is becoming more common, it is often low paid in relation to full-time work. Some employers still find it difficult to accept workers seriously unless they are at their desks for the whole working week. There are many positive exceptions, and perceptions are changing, but many people find it difficult to realise as good a wage, *pro rata*, working part time as they could full time.

Permanent employment

This means you have a contract of permanent employment, and you are protected by employment legislation to a greater degree than if you are temporary. It means that your employer cannot sack you without good grounds, and if you are made redundant, must pay you a set amount depending on how long you have worked in that company. There are advantages all round: workers who feel more secure, and that they 'belong' to an organisation, are often happier and so work better. The workplace community builds better with a permanent workforce. Workers feel secure to make life decisions such as buying a home or starting a family.

The problem is that there really is no job security any more, however black the ink on the contract. Redundancy is commonplace and sackings are not that uncommon either. People tend to feel more secure with a permanent contract, and are relatively secure, but are often shocked when what they felt was 'employment for life' comes to an abrupt end. People who can see work in this changing context tend to forge happier careers, it is thought, than people who cling on to an employer for grim life when that loyalty may not be repaid.

Temporary employment

This is another growing area. Many employers feel they can recruit the staff they need, as they need them, and so do not have to pay them when times are slack. The other perspective is that skilled workers, who can pick and choose where they work, may only sign temporary contracts, which they can then renegotiate at regular intervals. Who are the winners? It depends how skilled the workers are, and how much demand there is for those skills.

Unpaid work

People are not always available for paid work. This may be because they are caring for younger or older people, or those who are ill or have disabilities. They are still working but not being recognised for it statistically or financially. Others, who are unemployed but available for work often take on voluntary, unpaid work to help the community in some way, and to gain skills that will help them into paid work.

Voluntary work is also undertaken on a part-time basis by people who do have other, paid work. It forms an enormous slice of the work undertaken in the UK, although it is often overlooked as an option, and for what it gives the people who do it.

Unemployment

There is not always paid work of the right type available, and some people do not work. This is sometimes through choice. Usually it is because there is simply not the work for those people: they have the 'wrong' skills mix, or are the 'wrong' age, or have the 'wrong' experience. There are plenty of reasons why people find themselves out of work. Some of them go on to start their own businesses, while others prefer to continue to look for employment.

Franchising

You may want to start a business but keep the risks relatively low, or you may be short of ideas, or you may want to be part of a larger organisation. Franchising means buying the idea, and sometimes the equipment and stock, often the advertising and central expertise, from a franchise holder. Fast food outlets are often franchises – they are separate businesses, but follow a set pattern. To buy into a franchise, there is usually a substantial investment requirement for the high-street names, although some businesses can be started in this way with relatively low start-up costs.

Portfolio working

This a mix-and-match of different work patterns, and is becoming increasingly common. It's a return to pre-industrial working, in that you might have a mix, say, of a small business, a part-time job, community work and some caring. Elements of many of the patterns described above apply equally to employment and self-employment. For instance, if you set up a business with a partner, you could do so on a job-share basis; you may have a portfolio career involving a business, and so on.

SKILLS

Skills are our basic tools for life. They enable us to do all sorts of things, from tying shoelaces to running the country. We all have skills, and each of us has different skills in varying proportions. We all need skills, and people working in self-employment need skills specific to that, as well as more general ones.

Our attitudes and personalities can be referred to as skills: employers want workers who fit in, who turn up to work on time, who are positive about what they do. People in business need to be self-motivated and positive, well-grounded and full of ideas. Skills of this type are not easy to measure, or even define, while others are very specific and can be measured in tests or exams.

Experience

We divide skills into separate areas but really they all muddle up together inside us, making our own unique work potential. We tend to have more skills than we recognise. Also, we gain skills as we go – that is what 'experience' is all about: using what we do in life and work to develop additional skills. To start with, we need basic skills, both socially and in work. As well as these, the workplace requires certain general or 'transferable skills'. We need these wherever we work and whatever work we do. Other skills are more specific to a particular job or industry – these may be called employment skills. People label sets of skills differently, and it doesn't really matter what we call them, just that we understand the ideas behind the different types and why we need them.

Basic skills

These are skills such as being able to listen and speak in English, and to write and use language and numbers at a basic level, but well enough to make us competent in general social and work situations. They are also a base-level of abilities that allow us to gain other skills. For instance, if we have a horror of numbers and really don't understand them, we can't move on to statistical analysis; if we can't communicate effectively we can't absorb training in the workplace.

Transferable skills

These are more advanced basic skills, plus a whole range of abilities that make us good workers. They encompass general technical skills, as well as the attitudes and ambitions needed in any workplace. If we have these skills we can transfer them to any work situation.

Employment skills

These are skills specific to a work area, combined with the amalgam of basic and transferable skills you had before you trained for that work. This entire package forms your employment skills for a certain type of work. When you move into a new type of work, you take all your previous employment skills, and add new ones during your time in that new work. Some of these new ones become your transferable skills when you later move into more new work.

GAINING SKILLS

Some skills rub off on us as we do our work: we glean from others and so become more able ourselves. Some skills are taught to us, either socially or in education or training. Chapter 3 looks in more detail at gaining the skills you need for self-employment.

> *'I've been making clothes all the time since I left college. I sometimes think "what am I doing, just making things?" But I did a pattern-cutting course, and I've learnt a lot in technique, and I've got quite a few contacts. Things have come into place a lot, though.'* Ruth

Commentators describe ways of approaching the developing workplace: people who have difficulties in gaining recognised skills are thought to have less employment chances for the future; the willingness to learn in unsystematic ways is likely to become increasingly important; newer, unstructured learning approaches within the workplace will require high levels of self-discipline and organisation.

MAKING THE DECISION

Becoming self-employed may be a natural transition, or it may be the hardest decision you ever make. Some people have brilliant business ideas all their lives but never kick-start them into action. Others know they want to be self-employed but haven't yet found the specific business idea. Sometimes, everything seems to fall into place, and then comes the decision point. Maybe this comes:

- while still in compulsory education;
- on leaving school or college;
- when you return from travelling;
- when you are fed up with your current career;
- when you have gained the skills you need from your current work;
- when somebody asks to go into partnership with you;

- when you lose your job and feel you have no option but to try self-employment.

There are many possibilities. As in all things, if you have thought about it beforehand, and prepared for it, it is a relatively easy decision to make. If you haven't started working on the skills you might need, it is much harder.

You probably aren't at a decision point right now. That doesn't mean you can put this book down! The self-employment workplace is beckoning. One day you will need to think about it, perhaps very seriously, and when you do it'll be great to have had a head start.

Not a once-and–for-all decision

There are loads of inbetweeny things you can do: you don't have to commit the rest of your life to one thing now. Lives, and careers, move on. Self-employment may come and go within yours.

> 'I've always wanted to run my own business. I like being my own boss and believe that the only way to complete financial independence is by doing it all yourself. When I was 16 or 17 I worked in hotels, I'm fully silver-service trained. I was going to do a degree in hotel management, but it didn't work out. I did an A-level in law and went into the legal profession. I got bored of that, I wanted more out of life. I ended up doing a stint with Butlins and then became self-employed as a direct salesperson.' James

You may dabble, give up, dabble again, get bought out, do something part time, go back to full-time employment... It's understanding the possibilities that is important: possibilities in the workplace and possibilities within you.

An important part of this book is the virtual action plan (called Virtually There, on page 50). It is a way of looking at your ideas for self-employment in 'business-speak', to see whether you:

- have a thorough understanding of what you want to do;
- know how you would do it;
- know that it would work.

16

Most people looking at this action plan will come away thinking: 'No, I'm not ready yet!' That's great, because it underlines how much more research, thinking and skills-development there are still to accomplish. Try it time and again, and perhaps one day you'll find that things really are falling into place, and you can see a workable business idea emerging.

Chapter 2
EDUCATION

'You don't need any qualifications to run a business – it's all in the person you are and the skills you get as you go.' Peter, experienced businessman

If that's true, why bother with education? This section asks – and tries to answer – that question.

WHY BOTHER WITH EDUCATION?

'My education was no use for business. The only person who actually taught me anything in my fine art degree was the woodwork technician.' Ruth

'I was never taught anything useful. I've got a very low opinion of the whole school and college and university system, for what I do anyway. At school I wasn't able to do computers because I wasn't in the top set for maths. But I was doing a load of cool stuff at home.' Jim

Many people who have an entrepreneurial attitude to life – who want to get out there and do their own thing – feel this way about our relatively rigid education system. We have to go to school until we have taken our GCSEs, but is there any point? And if not, why not leave education then, and get some 'life experience' rather than wasting more time in class?

There are several answers to these questions.

Core skills

'There are the core skills that you've got to get hold of.' Tim

There are certain key, or core, skills that we all need, in employment and self-employment: numeracy, literacy, communication skills, and so on.

The essence of your future business may be in your sales skills and your product or service, but you also need to proofread your publicity material, total your invoices and keep your records up to date. Tedious, but necessary. There is more provision for adult literacy and numeracy classes these days, for those who have missed out, but will you really want to, or have the time to, go back to college in five or ten years' time?

School subjects are broadening. GNVQ qualifications have many advantages if you are thinking of going into business in some way. They are modular, and include key skills elements. You can leave half-way through a course and still have some proof of learning (but things are continually changing, so check this before you sign up). They are in vocational areas, which you can match to what you want to do. And the more academic school subjects (traditionally taught as A-levels) are being broadened with a new emphasis on AS-levels, giving sixth formers a wider learning base and so more flexibility. There should be something relevant and useful there for everyone.

Contacts

> *'Where will you get your contacts? Maybe it helps to have the right sort of people around you.'* Tim

If you are expecting your English teacher to help you set up in business as a cleaning contractor, you are probably expecting too much. But if you are studying subjects in vocational areas, or business studies, or have decided to study at a college specialising in a certain skills or work area, the people you mix with will have useful ideas, contacts and advice. And where else do you start? There are other places, but these contacts are being given to you on a plate.

Business awareness

> *'Some sort of business studies gives you some sort of idea of what you are going to do.'* Sixth form tutor

> *'I was educated at the London College of Printing. While doing my MA I did various business modules. A business education is extremely important, though it's no substitute for learning on-the-job. The theory*

19

equipped me to deal with the cynics. For example, I was able to pitch back at marketing and advertising people.' Matt

Why not take what is being offered? There are specific courses offered by enterprise agencies and other organisations, but these probably aren't yet suitable as they are aimed at people ready to get started in business. Are you ready? Do you have any saleable skills yet? Is setting up in self-employment going to work now? It's traditional to see 'business' as something done by older people, who have already gained education and/or experience. Attitudes are changing to this, and there is much more emphasis on 'enterprise' from earlier on, but these are still important questions. Unless you know you are ready, why not take what is on offer, and learn all you can about business, or a subject area, or just enjoy learning?

Some degrees and HNDs attract commercial sponsors, who pay students to study. These graduates are then ready for work in that organisation. Even courses such as the postgraduate MBA (Master of Business Administration) have traditionally been geared to training managers for work in large organisations. The emphasis is now changing, and some MBAs, for instance, have options directed at people looking to start their own businesses. One sixth of all UK undergraduates are now on business-related courses. Education is changing at every level. The more you can take from it, while it is being offered, the better.

Fallback

You may want or need a job at some point. Recruiters are fussy people: they look at qualifications. They want to see that you were committed to something (your education) and worked hard at it, so that they can believe you will be committed and work hard for them. You are at school or college anyway; why not use that time to get decent grades? You are young; why not spend a couple more years in education and get qualifications that will convince others that you're capable of work? This isn't always the right path, but if it's possible for you, go for it. Many, many young people who leave school early because they want to get into work, and to get earning and experienced, fall too easily into low-paid dead-end work because they are not qualified, and their education and employment record is not impressive. This is fine if your business never looks back, but most entrepreneurs spend some time in employment. Making sure you are employable is common sense.

WHEN TO LEAVE EDUCATION

It's true that some people do leave education relatively early, for all sorts of different reasons, and make a great success of their working lives. Some people believe it's better to be getting real-life experience than learning irrelevant things in school or college. That might be true for you. But some education is both academic and work-oriented (vocational), and leaves choices open.

It depends if you see yourself as a more prudent type, who assesses the options and progresses in a measured way, or more of a mover, ready to go out now and start this thing you have been waiting to do for so long.

Some people do both, and set up in business while at college, but people who do too much paid work (rather than study) during their college years suffer academically. There's little point spending a number of years studying then failing to get the qualification at the end of it.

Does it matter whether you get academic qualifications?

'When you haven't got any work you can show people when you start up, the initials you can put on your business card and flyers mean a lot. And to some people, they continue to be important.' Tim

In business, people want you to deliver what you promise. They don't care whether you have an MBA or a few poor GCSEs – they want the result. Sometimes, though, the sales process – convincing them that yes, you can deliver the goods or service they want – requires proof. It may make no difference whether you have a degree or not – what customers want is a level of assurance that you can deliver, and initials after your name may offer this.

Other things can offer it too: the recommendation of a colleague or friend is a great way to get business, and customers often choose goods or services this way. But when you start out, and later on where the buying criteria are rigid, certain qualifications are necessary, or at least helpful.

How do you make the decision to leave education?

Who can say, but you? Make sure you talk to lots of people first, and get a good idea of what you are doing. It is possible to get back into the education system, and this is becoming usual at the higher education stage, but it's a lot easier to go along with your peers and do it at the usual time.

FURTHER AND HIGHER EDUCATION

'At Kerb we've all got degrees or MAs but everyone has these days – it's so easy to get a degree. But someone who's sat and worked out the software at home is worth a lot more than someone with three years' tuition.' Jim

More and more people get degrees, but you don't need a degree to run a business. A degree used to mean something purely academic. Now it often ties the vocational with the academic, and gives you a chance to get some of the work experience you need for employment or becoming self-employed.

The new universities offer plenty of vocational 'sandwich' course HNDs and degrees. (An HND is at roughly the same level as a degree – a 'smaller' degree, taken over two years, often including work experience. You may be able convert it to a degree with an extra year at the end.) These can be thin or thick sandwiches (meaning more or less time in work experience; different timing for this, and so on) and they come in a gigantic range of subjects and options.

Choosing your course

You need the *UCAS Handbook* and companion volumes written to clarify choice at this level. It is also invaluable to speak to people in the sort of work you are considering, and ask them what they think. Talk to admissions tutors, too. Ask them what happens to their graduates: what sort of work they go in to, how employable they are.

Careers teachers and advisers should be able to help, though if you are looking at specialist areas, they may have to go and find out for you. They may refer you to one of the specialist careers programmes available on the college or careers service computers. These can help you narrow down your choices by asking questions about you, and what you want to do. Others provide information on the courses available.

What experience to get while at college/university

Education is a 'place' for being taught... it is also a place to spread wings, to try new things, to think independently, and to pick up skills for the workplace. If that workplace is going to involve self-employment, it's possible that you will be dabbling in it already, or starting fairly soon.

> *'At university the teachers didn't understand the subjects being taught. But the degree was really good because it gave me the freedom to do what I wanted to do. In my last year at university they were really cool and let me do a load of commercial stuff. I did a degree in Electronic Media, mainly 3D animation. In my final year I was doing loads and loads of business.'* Jim

Gaining experience is covered under the next section, but while you're thinking about education, remember that it can provide:

- **Long vacations.** Vacations may mean slaving away in a factory or restaurant kitchen just to make your loan stretch to the end of the year, but what if they could mean setting up a small trading business instead, or at the same time?

- **Access to resources you couldn't otherwise afford.** *'If you study art subjects, it gives you time to do what you want, lots of other people to feed off. And you can use school or college equipment and software,'* says Jim. The same applies in other areas too, of course.

- **Other people's brains.** Ideas, and 'people to feed off,' as Jim says. People to contradict you, tease your ideas into something practical, workable, viable.

- **Enterprise skills.** Learning methods at university encourage self-motivation and self-starting. Government-funded initiatives within universities aim to encourage these enterprise and workplace skills.

- **Potential business partners.** How many people end up working with people they meet at college? The friends and contacts you make there often last a lifetime.

- **Contacts.** Not just business partners but mentors and other people who will support your enterprise.

- **A ready base of customers.** If you plan to dabble a little while still at college, you have a ready-made client base. They don't have much spare cash, but that makes targeting and marketing all the more interesting. Practice on your fellow-students – or their parents, your tutors, or another group outside the establishment – and set up a business aimed at them. You may be able to do this within an enterprise initiative set up by your university or union, and may be able to get business advice from your enterprise or other agency.

What to study

Here are some examples of what you can study.

At GCSE stage...

Get the basics behind you: English, maths, a language or two if you can, the basics of science, and so on. You will be encouraged to keep your learning broad, even if you are not a natural genius in each of these areas. If you study GNVQs, basic key skills are built into your qualification: communication, application of number, and ICT (information and communications technology).

In further education

Here is a selection of vocational and business study that you can do at school and in further education (this is the level of study people are usually doing between the ages of 16 and 19):

- GCSEs in any of the subjects you fluffed or missed out on;
- A-levels in the academic subjects, plus business studies;
- AS-levels in other related subjects, especially now that the educational emphasis is shifting towards having a broader sixth form subject base;
- GNVQs in business and other vocational subjects. These *'develop the knowledge, understanding and skills needed for work in broad occupational areas like business, manufacturing and retail & distributive services'* (DfEE website).

At university...

'If you've got a business degree you know all there is to know about running a business. While at college I ran a young enterprise company, so I got to know how to run a business.' Christos

'I did a fine art degree, and since then I've been teaching myself, and learning, and refining my ideas on making my clothes, for the last two and half years. On a fine art course you don't know anything about the outside world. On most fashion courses you do a placement for a year, it's more integral to the course, showing your sketchbooks to people, getting into the whole fashion world.' Ruth

Go through the *UCAS Handbook* and pick out a few goodies:

- Business studies, as a main subject or paired with all sorts of things
- Business administration
- Business information
- Office studies
- Hospitality management
- Small business enterprise
- Environmental business studies
- European business studies
- Rural business management
- All the accountancy degrees
- Anything combining your area of interest with a business element.

These are simply degree and HND course titles taken at random. Even within courses of the same name, the content and emphasis will differ. You can't make up your mind about which course to do without reading through the relevant prospectuses, reading around the subject (with alternative guides to universities, for instance) and hopefully visiting and speaking to the tutors.

You can choose to do some of these as sandwich courses (which combine academic study with a practical training and business experience) by working for an employer during a year away from the course. Sandwich courses come in different formats. Some involve sponsorship, where the employer pays you to study, and may ask for a commitment to work for them after the degree course.

After university

The most common business qualification at postgraduate level is the MBA – the Master of Business Administration. It is a year's study full-time, and is often taken after gaining work experience. Large employers may sponsor their managers to take this full or part time. It is more for the manager in a corporation than the small trader, though less so now, and the subjects can be applied to both.

Other postgraduate qualifications are more specific to certain areas, and there is of course a huge range of professional qualifications, taken while working. These are considered 'training' rather than 'education' and come in the next chapter.

CHECKLIST

Go through these points to:

- work out your options;
- see how close you are to making a decision.

1. Do you know what you still need to learn, and whether you plan to stay in education? If not:

- Read up about business.
- Read up about your area of interest.
- Talk to people already doing further study, and people in business – what do they think about more education?

> 'From an art-based point of view, I would advise people not to do a fine art degree. Do more practical-based things. I was into conceptual ideas of art – I would advise people to spend their spare time doing that. You can read books, form your own ideas of philosophy, you don't need to be taught it. They should do something arts-based but actually learn skills, so they've got something behind them. I don't regret it as I got a lot out of it but if I could go back and do it again, I would do fashion, probably, or a furniture course. I like the idea of learning a real skill.' Ruth

- Don't listen to one person – get an overview from a number of people in different situations. Remember that times have changed and that higher education is much more widely gained – and required – than when some older people were at your stage.

■ Find out exactly what you lack, in terms of necessary qualifications; specific industry skills; enterprise skills (see Chapter 3).

Then look at:

2. How are you going to learn it? This may be through:

■ experience/training in employment;
■ part-time work/self-employment plus study;
■ specific enterprise courses after leaving education and while working;
■ full-time education.

3. If it is in full-time education:

■ research all the possible options and courses;
■ talk to as many people as possible about them;
■ be proactive – phone the university, ask questions, be assertive;
■ recognise that if you do go ahead with a degree/HND, you will need to make it a total commitment.

If you are unsure, and you are running out of time and need to make a decision, the general feeling is that it is better to be more highly educated. If you still don't know, take a year off to think about it. If you're getting to the end of that year... do you:

■ make a leap into a further education/degree/HND course?
■ go into work and training?
■ set up in business now?

The undecided are usually also uncommitted: don't go into business because you can't think what else to do. Successful entrepreneurs need all the motivation they can find, and more. Read the rest of this book first, keep talking to people, go on courses, research and network wherever you go.

Chapter 3
SKILLS, EXPERIENCE & TRAINING

What do we sell when we are self-employed?

Our skills. We either:

- sell these direct, eg when we do someone's garden for them;
- use them to create a product;
- use them to manage a team which creates a product; and so on.

These are our specific, industry or sector related skills. Yet any employment requires skills. Self-employed people say that they need more skills than employees, and it's certainly true that we need a wide range of them – we use additional skills to run the business itself. There are lots of these, things like:

- administrative skills;
- idea generation;
- common sense;
- marketing skills
- picking-ourselves-off-the-floor-and-starting-again skills.

There is also knowledge, both of our industry/trade/profession, and of the world of business. We need a great deal of knowledge about self-employment before we can set up in that way. Although the knowledge itself isn't exactly a skill, knowing how to discover it is. This section isn't about knowledge itself. This can be gleaned from the final section of the book and independent research. Here we look again at the skills mentioned in the first section of this book. This section looks in more detail at skills, and at gaining skills. It covers:

- which skills we need;
- when to obtain these skills, and how;
- a skills portfolio.

IDENTIFYING THE RIGHT SKILLS TO DEVELOP

'You need to be really good at a skill to set up a business. My skill really is my imagination, and secondary to that is my sewing, which is the formula for bringing the imagination out. That's why I'm building that up at the moment.' Ruth

If you are planning an organised approach to gaining skills, it makes sense to:

- isolate the skills you are likely to need;
- tick off the ones you already have;
- work out how to get the ones you are lacking.

Not everyone approaches work 'in advance' in this way: plenty of people wait for opportunities to come to them, and then act. That's fine; but just think how much simpler, and possibly more successful, things will be if you can pre-empt the opportunity. If you get those skills into place now, you will be prepared for setting up in self-employment when the time and opportunity are right.

How you organise this process is up to you. Some people keep everything filed neatly in their portable filing systems: their heads. Others have a notebook or more literal file. Find the best way for you, but at least have a think about the process of getting prepared.

THE SKILLS YOU NEED

(NB different people put different labels on these groups of skills: their classification isn't important, though the idea behind them is.)

Basic skills

These are the key or core skills:

- numeracy;
- literacy;
- ICT (information and communications technology);
- communication skills.

They are a foundation for anything we do in life. The ICT element is fairly recent and doesn't yet apply to every situation we find ourselves in, but in time it will.

Transferable skills

These are the ones that we learn then take into any work (and social) situation. They are not specifically about one type of work, but necessary for all work. We don't need to be perfect in every area of each but do need to develop them as we continue in our working lives. Some employers and businesses will tolerate less-that-perfect skills of one type; other employers and businesses demand perfection in those, but not in others. For instance, it might be crucial that we turn up for work a few minutes early and are in place exactly on time. In other work situations it may not matter. But in general it will help working life enormously if we have the discipline to do that, whatever is finally required of us.

Here are some examples of transferable skills:

initiative	self-motivation
team-working	planning
sense of humour	dedication
decision-making	loyalty
time-management	ambition
creativity	self-reliance
patience	reliability
persistence	punctuality
empathy	driving skills
good memory	basic keyboard skills
efficiency	other basic technical skills

The list is much, much longer. Really, they cover many of our positive attributes, plus any more that we could do with acquiring. They make us into rounded, responsible people, and that makes us good at our work. The more of them we have, the better we will be able to cope with demanding work… and being self-employed is very demanding.

Employment skills

These are everything, all lumped together, that enable you to work in a certain area, and they include skills specific to that area. They include:

Basic skills
Such as numeracy to enable you to check deliveries to delivery notes and invoices; and literacy to be able to read and interpret the invoices, to write business letters etc.

Transferable skills
To help you mix with clients and prospective clients, to help you work in any environment, and so on – patience, all-weather working, problem-solving, security etc.

Industry-specific skills
These are the ones that tie in with your area of work, or interest in work. For instance, if you enjoy woodwork, you might consider a career as a joiner, and might hope to be self-employed as a way of organising this work. Your skills list might include: advanced woodworking and joinery, estimating in your specific area, buying the joinery materials you need, subcontracting, and so on.

Enterprise skills
These are relevant to people setting up in self-employment – which means you. This is because, if the crystal ball is right, most of us will work as self-employed people at some stage in our lives. Enterprise skills overlap with many of the other types, but it's worth thinking about them separately as well. As a self-employed joiner, or importer, or ICT consultant, which of these would you need?

Sales skills:	Understanding how people tick
	Communicating with them
	'Closing', ie asking for/getting the contract
Management skills:	Leadership
	Planning
	Decision-making

	Personal and general responsibility
Administrative skills:	Prioritising
	Organising
	Book-keeping
	Knowing the legalities
Looking ahead:	Continuing to learn
	Open-mindedness
Ideas and pazzazz:	Finding new opportunities and ideas
	Problem-solving
	Original thinking, lateral thinking
	Objectivity
	Ambition
	Risk-taking
'Industry', or hard work:	Working long hours
	Doing every job yourself
	Flexibility

There are many, many enterprise skills. Enterprise, or self-employment, and the skills necessary to it, becomes a way of life, and becomes part of the people we are, rather than being a mix of isolated skills that we acquire here and there. Getting a 'feel' for the process of self-employment, and what it entails, is by far the best way of understanding the skills it demands. This is an overview of them, but what we need is to research, to go and speak with people in self-employment, and to watch them at work. Their skills will soon become apparent.

As we do this we can form our skills listing, and look more closely at those skills we feel we already have, and those we lack. It is a gradual process, and that is fine. Any business adviser or mentor will say: take your time. Start early, with vacation or weekend self-employment or work, and build on that. Or go into employment and gain skills there, while also thinking about enterprise skills, and making sure we glean them as we can, as we go.

NATURE VS NURTURE: PERSONAL CHARACTERISTICS

This is always a good topic for a heated conversation: are we the product of our genes, or of the way we are brought up? Whatever your view, there is consensus that entrepreneurs need certain personal characteristics.

> *'We're both determined, and prepared to put the time in, and we both expect to make a go of it.'* Christos

> *'You have to be able to see the big picture and have faith in what you're doing, you do get tremendous knock-backs. You can't be affected by short-term problems. You need a sense of humour.'* Matt

> *'With your own business you've got to be prepared to put 110% in, until you're successful enough to step back a bit.'* Emma

> *'You need a whole lot of determination, because it's not the easy way out. You can be working from seven in the morning to two the next morning and not earning a penny for it. You reap the proceeds at a later date.'* James

> *'I've always had a natural flair with people.'* James

> *'To run a business you have to be really, really organised and be an administrator.'* Jim

> *'You have to have personality and determination and ability to get through.'* Tim

Whether you were born with them or learned them during your upbringing, you need to weigh up whether you have the intrinsic qualities necessary to cope with the pressures of self-employment. After that, you need to assess the areas where you do not, and act upon them.

> *'My sales training helped, it enhanced my natural character. You need good communication skills – I got these from the legal profession. I'm quite a precise person so I've had to let myself go a little bit, change my style a bit, get into the real world a bit more.'* James

There is always scope to learn and change: once we know where we are heading and have assessed the obstacles and understand the routes, we can work on making the necessary changes: working on ourselves to develop the characteristics that make a successful entrepreneur.

WHEN, WHERE AND HOW TO DEVELOP SKILLS

People talk about the 'university of life' – meaning that the important things we learn come from our life experience, not our formal education. Others rate the 'education' part more highly. As in most things, it's a mix-and-match according to the people we are and the backgrounds we have.

- We can choose to attend school only up until our sixteenth birthdays, and then settle back and never learn anything else in formal education (or elsewhere).
- We can see the whole of life as a learning experience, and make a point of getting what we can from it.

Education

We undoubtedly learn an enormous amount through our infancy and childhood. We continue to learn through our adolescence and schooling, through our extracurricular activities and friendships, through all our relationships. Education is designed to give us:

- skills – 'key' skills, as already noted, plus many additional ones;
- knowledge – it enables us to participate in trivia quizzes even if the knowledge we gain seems, sometimes, a little irrelevant;
- qualifications – which may seem pointless, but for most people come in handy at some time or other;
- a platform for the rest of life – something to jump off from, a good grounding;
- an introduction to further learning;
- an introduction to work;
- contacts – friendships, mentors, perhaps more.

Broadly, education lasts as long as we want it to, and gives us what we demand from it. It can continue right through life, and indeed, this is becoming more commonplace, and increasingly recognised in government policy.

Training schemes

Once education leaves the classroom and ties in with work, we call it training. Training can mean all sorts of things, from doing day-centre voluntary work with a half hour's informal briefing beforehand about how to serve the meals, to training for a professional qualification over a number of years while also working to gain experience.

Training can be:
- on-the-job: you do the work and a trainer supervises and instructs;
- off-the-job: you leave the workplace, or give up your own time, to learn about your work in a classroom situation.

It can be:
- a training scheme devised by your employer;
- a training scheme devised by the government (through an agency such as the JobCentre or Enterprise Agency);
- a training scheme devised by you;
and financed by any of these parties, in any combination.

It can be:
- relatively full time;
- relatively low key, in terms of time commitment.

It can be:
- for a specified length of time, short or long;
- a commitment to ongoing training.

It can be:
- age-related (such as the New Deal initiative);
- task-related (an employer needs you and trains you to satisfy that need);
- you-related (you decide that you need training, and go out and get it).

There are limitless variations: training cannot mean just one thing, given the vast range of people and the occupations they do. But all training has one thing in common – it develops skills.

Experience

Education and training alone are not enough to give us the skills to prepare us to do a job. Experience also develops skills.

Training really means: 'education with experience'. But you can get experience without any training, and if you look at it the right way and see what it can do for you, it can be useful. Examples of this include many of the low-paid jobs we do for extra cash while at school, college and university. We may be asked to clear out gutters or take a dog for a walk. It is always useful to be given some training to do these tasks, but often we are just given the task and it is assumed that we know how to do it. Tasks such as these can give us a variety of skills, eg:

- reliability
- initiative
- perseverance
- ladder-juggling
- navigating, and so on.

Life experience also counts in gaining skills: the bust-up we have with a friend, for instance, teaches us how to handle difficult situations, and cope with people.

In reality though, with so much emphasis on training for young people, whether through government schemes or employer programmes, most experience you gain through work will be via a planned training scheme, and you'll find the 'training' and 'experience' elements blend in together, at least when you first start work. The other times of life to develop experience (outside training schemes) are before leaving education, and after the initial 'youth training' phase of employment. The latter is for looking at later in life and work. This next section looks at gaining experience (and skills) outside formal training schemes.

GAINING EXPERIENCE

'If you can get work experience, go for it, it helps.' Christos

Here are some ways to isolate, and then gain, skills before taking the leap and becoming a trainee or full-time self-employed:

- weekend-type jobs while at school and college;
- participation in enterprise clubs and programmes organised by your institution;
- work experience (*'Anna had done a year's work experience in her degree, and learned the nitty gritty of having your own label'* Christos);
- holiday and vacation work, sandwich/gap year work;
- finding a mentor;
- early 'non-career' jobs;
- setting up a small business while still in education, or alongside employment (*'We had orders prior to setting up, as Anna had been working freelance and had orders from friends and family'* Christos);
- specific education (such as a business degree specialising in small-business management);
- specific courses on self-employment.

Weekend-type jobs while at school and college

'I do a Sunday job in a newsagent and get enough cash to get me through the week.' Sixth-form student

The usual teenage reason to do weekend work is to earn enough money to enjoy a good social life or pursue a particular hobby. If this is what you already do, think around your work, and the tasks you are doing, and try listing the skills you are gaining each time you go to work. The chances are that it won't be very interesting work (though it is often what we make of it). You might include skills such as:

- till work
- mental arithmetic
- working with people
- keeping polite and cheerful all day
- customer relations
- learning the newspaper and confectionery trade, and so on.

If you never learned how to get yourself out of bed on time, this is when it starts happening. If you used to chuck study when it got too boring, maybe your perseverance here (for a more immediate reward – the pay) is good training.

Maybe you haven't done any of this type of work – is it time to give it a try? Even a couple of hours a week can change our views on what work is, whether we want to work for someone else, how we might prefer to work, and so on.

Participation in enterprise clubs and programmes

Schools and colleges often have clubs or associations to give students information and experience in a safe environment. There is usually a commercial project in which you can take part. This sort of activity involves you right from the beginning, and can get you to the 'top' – being the big boss.

> *'I'm a director of "Munchies". We open every Thursday lunchtime selling snacks to students on campus. It's good most of the time but we have personality clashes. I've nearly chucked it in a few times but I want to stick it to see if I can.'* FE college student

You will be gaining all sorts of useful skills here. This type of activity might also make you think about:

Your management style

Do you enjoy taking over and running the whole thing? Does that cause problems with others? How do you cope with this? Are you democratic or authoritarian? Are you keen to be involved but want to do it in a quieter way? Are you better at getting a team to work well together from behind the scenes than actually leading it? Does one particular business function suit you better than others?

What is entailed in running a business?

More than meets the eye. Although you won't get bogged down in regulation and legislation, there will still be basic health and safety rules. The books need keeping properly, and accounts presented at the end of the trading year. Have you made a profit? How do you distribute it?

All these issues make us think about enterprise. Think too about skills, and keep noting where you perform well, and where you are floundering. Which bits do you enjoy more than others? As a package, is it appealing? Can you imagine doing it 60 hours a week, year after year?

Work experience

Why not try to arrange work experience, or work shadowing, in a small business or with a freelance? It's a good way of learning some of the realities of self-employment.

Holiday and vacation work; sandwich/gap year work

This is more concentrated than part-time work in term-time, and more of a taster of what work can be like. It's a good idea to try to do different types of work. If you find an employer who will offer you continuing vacation work, and pays you well, it's hard to think about giving that up. Perhaps you could talk to your manager about your experience needs, and see whether you could move around in the organisation. Perhaps that person would become your mentor (see below).

Holiday/vacation work can be:

- at many different grades and in any field;
- simply to stretch your pocket money or loan;
- to gain experience;
- part of a sandwich course at university – your vacation work will be organised for you as a part of your sandwich, and will be relevant to your degree and the work your sponsor hopes you will do in that organisation afterwards.

However your work pans out, continue to observe:

- the structure of the organisation;
- the way people work together;
- the different levels of staff and how they relate.

Add to this:

- how you fit in;
- what you enjoy more, and less;
- what you are best at.

Can you see how well the organisation is being run? Could you do it better? Do you have the skills to do that? What additional skills would you first need to gain?

Finding a mentor

Mentors are people who watch over us, and our progress, in a particular area: form or personal tutors at school or college are a type of mentor. They are experienced people, whom we can trust, and who can advise us on how to progress. Sometimes we have mentors in-built into our family or social lives, or into our training schemes. Maybe we need to go out and look for one. They can give:

- advice;
- support;
- problem-solving help;
- contacts; and more.

If you already know someone who you can ask for help, why not ask whether they might be prepared to be your mentor in a slightly more formal way? Maybe you could ask whether they would meet you every three months, say, and look at your plans for your business, or at your skills development, or whatever it is you would like from them.

> *'We still see our mentor once a month, he goes through our accounts. It's nice to keep in touch, that way you've got someone to guide you.'*
> Christos

Check with your parents, if appropriate, before forming any relationship with an older person in this way, and in any event, use your developing people-awareness skills to ensure your own personal safety.

Sometimes, mentors come in-built into schemes, especially those that rely on people learning from experience rather than books. New entrepreneurs with the Prince's Youth Business Trust, for instance, are allocated a mentor to guide them through the preparation of a business plan and to question every assumption they make: it is a useful way of assessing the feasibility of ideas, in the light of a more experienced person's views.

Mentors shouldn't tell you what to do. They should be able to point out areas where they feel you are not thinking straight, or where you do not have the skills to make a project work, say.

Early 'non-career' jobs

Many of us start our brilliant careers in unskilled, low-paid work, or in voluntary work. This can be despite the best education. Sometimes these jobs lead up the ladder into management, for example, but often they are just fill-ins, to pay the rent, to pass the time until a job comes up in the 'right' industry. In some areas, especially the glamorous occupations such as parts of the media or film industries, you are expected to scratch around doing 'work experience' for a while – perhaps it is seen as 'character-building', or maybe it simply feeds free labour into the system.

These experiences can be frustrating. They are increasingly common, so if you find yourself doing it, don't despair: new directions do come along. In the meantime, what can you be doing to make the best use of the experience you are getting?

As described above, you can be:

- examining the skills you are gaining;
- evaluating the way the organisation works;
- thinking how it could be improved;
- matching yourself to it: would you run it any better? How? If the answer is: 'not yet', then what do you need to learn first? And how will you learn it?

Maybe you're not going to get the work experience you know you need right now: in that case, are there other ways of moving forward while still slaving to pay the rent? Perhaps the next few ideas will help.

Setting up a small business

You can do this while still in education, or alongside employment or unemployment.

> 'There's nothing to stop you putting an ad in Yellow Pages and waiting to see if the phone rings. If it does, go on from there.'

This is one approach – best used once we have some skills to sell. But in essence, this student is right: why not just bite the bullet and go for it? There's not a great deal to lose except a bit of advertising to be paid, time spent to set up a package worth selling, and to go and quote/sell your services. However, make sure it doesn't interfere with your other commitments; sixth formers who work more than five hours per week start to underperform in their studies, while those who work more than 15 hours per week can expect to see their A-level points score drop by up to 8 points.

Some entrepreneurs have several businesses on the go, and during the time one is busier (perhaps more seasonal than the others) they let the others die down a little. So why not do that alongside education or employment? The learning curve will be steep, but as long as we are honest about what we can do, or provide, the rewards will be worth having in terms of experience, if not financially.

Some enterprise agencies will see students, at least for an initial group session, so it's worth phoning around to see what help is available 'in advance'. If you are unemployed, the New Deal initiative (for people aged 18–24 and unemployed for six months or more) can offer a period of 'test trading'. After some training, you may be able to trade for up to six months while still a New Deal client and receiving benefits.

Specific education
(such as a business degree specialising in small-business management)

Look again at the previous section on education: use the research resources available to glean what you can about each course you're interested in. Think too about part-time degrees and diplomas, and whether you might fit one of those around other work as a preparation for self-employment.

Ask around: what workplace skills can 'book-learning' actually give you? Ask admissions tutors this question too. Do the answers satisfy you? Or might you do better gaining the skills you need during employment and training?

Specific courses on self-employment

There are government-funded agencies around the country, set up to promote enterprise. Some, such as Business Link, are designed to help existing businesses. Others, such as the Enterprise Agencies, help with start-up and early trading. Their help is either free or heavily subsidised. Other organisations work with different funding: the Prince's Youth Business Trust (PYBT), for instance, is a charity set up specifically to help young people with a disadvantaged background. Livewire is funded by a company, Shell, and helps young people setting up in business. It has an annual competition to find, applaud and reward young entrepreneurs.

These organisations, and others (see the Information section, page 64), offer initial advice free of charge, and may then suggest you attend a course or business advice session with them.

> 'It you've got a good idea, I strongly recommend the PYBT. As soon as they got involved they organised fashion shows for us and other fashion businesses in the area. If you think you have a potentially good business idea, seek advice, and if you're within the age group, go to PYBT, they will help you set up and go through it all with you.'
> Christos

They may put you in touch with a mentor, and guide you through the process of thinking through and developing, setting up and funding, then running, your business.

One enterprise agency, for instance, offers these courses:

- **Business Advice Sessions:** creating an awareness and understanding of the problems likely to be encountered when starting a business (free).

- **Market Research for Pre-Starts:** can you prove there is a market for your product or service, or do you just think there is? (£10).

43

- **Business Start-Up Workshops:** an A–Z of the requirements of starting a business (£20).

- **Business Finance & Accounts Seminar:** cashflow and finance are the backbone of your business. Keep financial control from day one (£10).

A SKILLS PORTFOLIO

We each have a cluster of skills, our 'skills portfolio'. It is unique to us and to what we do, and want to do. In the same way that everything: all organisations, entities, relationships, and so on – need to move on and grow, and need to have energy put into them, so do our skills. It's not enough to gain some then sit back and forget about skills development.

This chapter has looked at skills: defining them, working out which we need, and at the opportunities for developing them. As a checklist for our skills portfolio, we can ask ourselves questions such as:

- What skills do I already have?
- What work have I done to add to these?
- What have I gained from this, in terms of experience and knowledge?
- Am I ready to set up a business or to go freelance?

If you don't know the answer to the last question, or the answer is 'no', you don't know enough about skills, or about self-employment. If the answer is 'yes', perhaps you are ready for a session with an adviser, to see whether you really understand the processes – and pitfalls – of becoming self-employed.

Whichever way you go at this stage, here are a few points to think about:

- Keep a log of ideas/directions/skills needed/ways you might get those skills.
- Always think 'portfolio', never get tracked into one thing, one skill.
- Set yourself a target – gain one new skill a month/year etc.
- Keep doing it – experience is the best training for work.
- Look abroad, to the US and others who are 'ahead' of us – what new skills are they developing?

- Find people working in those fields and pick their brains.
- Do work for free if necessary, to keep skills going.
- Offer to develop projects, or manage them.
- Read trade journals, surf the web.

So... that was skills: now that we have them, what are we going to do with them? The next section is a practical one, looking at how to go about planning self-employment. It can also be approached as an enterprise 'game', so even if you don't yet feel ready to plan a real business, try it out and see where the ideas lead.

Chapter 4
DOING IT

There are planners, and there are doers. If you fail to plan, everything crashes around you. If you fail to act, then you are no entrepreneur. If you are a planner and a doer, you are on the entrepreneurial springboard.

The first parts of this book have been about planning and preparation. This section encourages you to focus on:

- where you are now;
- where you want to go; and
- how you plan to get there.

It is split into five parts:

1. A quiz to see if you are ready to become self-employed.
2. A lead-in to the information section that follows this chapter (information you may need in order to make the action plan, see 3 below).
3. An action plan called Virtually There. This is a way of devising your own business without the risk: doing it on paper and in your mind.
4. A review of this virtual business; an assessment of how well it suited you, and what you have learned for next time (for another virtual business, or perhaps this time, the Real Thing).
5. A summary, with a reminder of the realities of self-employment.

QUIZ: WHERE DO YOU STAND RIGHT NOW?

Use this quiz to:

- evaluate yourself now – your current feelings and your readiness for self-employment;
- consider how ready you might feel at a certain time in the future.

You may feel ready to become self-employed now, or the idea of becoming self-employed could seem decades away. However you feel, some sort of personal assessment is useful. Try this quiz now, and again at intervals. Your overall feeling by the end of this exercise may be: don't do it! Or it may start off that way and then change over time until it does feel right.

There are no 'correct' answers to this sort of self-evaluation: it's up to you to get a feel for where you are, after thinking about the questions. If you can't get that feel, perhaps you are not ready. You may not know the answers because you do not yet know enough about aspects such as business funding. So:

■ read through it anyway;
■ read part 3 of this section (the 'virtual' business plan);
■ read the alphabetical listing of business issues (page 64).

You might then find that you have enough knowledge to get more from the quiz.

Think about where you stand right now...

Emotionally

Are you:
■ emotionally secure – ready to take any knocks that come along, and still believe in yourself?
■ still not ready or independent enough to take that initiative and branch out on your own?
■ working towards more emotional readiness? How can you do this? Is it down to time? Experience? Listening? Acting? Trying and failing? What is the best way forward for you now?

Skills-wise

■ Are you aware of all your skills?
■ Which skills of what type do you have?
■ Where are you lacking in skills, both generally (in enterprise and work terms) and specifically for the area you want to set up in?
■ How are you going to gain these?
■ Do you have a master-plan down in writing, a way of steadily

progressing towards gaining these skills?

- What knowledge do you still need? How are you going to get this?
- Is your networking in place and ongoing? Is it useful? A good indication is the number of new ideas you get from talking to other people. How can you progress this?

Ambition and drive-wise

There are many successful management styles, and no 'correct' way of being self-employed. Some traits, however, are almost universal in successful self-employed people. Do you have these personal qualities to really make a go of it, or is it just wishful thinking? Can you successfully analyse yourself? What do your friends think? Your family? Ask yourself, and them, whether you are:

- clear-thinking, practical, level-headed, realistic;
- self-disciplined;
- determined;
- organised, or organised enough to delegate;
- a listener;
- happy to sell;
- hard-working.

There are many personal characteristics you need to be successful in business: which others can you think of? Where could you find a checklist?

Education-wise

- What stage are you at?
- Are you finished with education? Definitely? Maybe? For now?
- Are you planning more education? When? What? How? Will this take planning? And financing? Have you worked out how to finance it? Are your plans just ideas in your head or written and reviewed regularly?
- Are you open to changing your education plans if your ideas change? Are you keeping your education options open by making sure you get the grades you need in the exams you are already committed to?
- Do you have academic referees in place? Are these just the standard

anonymous scraps of paper or can you approach a tutor for a more personal recommendation?

Business-wise

Do you know:
- All there is to know about the theory of business? How can you learn more?
- What sort of self-employment you want to do: is it a certain type of work, or area of interest, that attracts you most, or is it the idea of working for yourself?
- How to generate ideas? Do you have one idea that must succeed at all costs, or can you think flexibly around this and look at other possibilities?
- How long is your ideas list? How often do you add to it?

Financially

Do you:
- Understand the financial risks of setting up on your own?
- Have a partner or sponsor to help you fund your business?
- Have financial security (such as equity in a property) to secure a loan?
- Know how much you need to live on day-to-day, and for the business in its different cycles? So, do you...
- Have a business plan (see page 50), and a personal financial profile (page 56) of all your financial needs?

Quiz conclusion

Did you know the answers to all those questions? Were they the 'right' answers, or do you need to go away, re-think and re-research? Self-employed people never stop thinking: if you want to do that, get a job! If you want to be successful in self-employment, recognise that there is always a learning curve. Are you happy about that?

> *'You're always learning new stuff, all the time. I am meeting up with people and learning. What I'm making now is so much better than a year ago. It's a long-scale thing for me.'* Ruth

ABOUT THE INFORMATION SECTION

The quiz should have raised more questions than it answered. There is a huge amount to know about self-employment – it bogs down the most able, motivated and experienced of us. This book can't hope to tell you everything but, for starters, the next section includes an alphabetical listing of some of the points we need to consider before launching into business (see page 64). It is a starting point for research, not an end-point. You might find is useful to look at this next, and keep it for future reference.

If you already know all of that, then carry on to the following section, which works through a business plan to give you some idea of the points you need to think about. Then look again at your answers, and the points you don't yet know.

VIRTUALLY THERE: DEVELOPING YOUR OWN BUSINESS PLAN

You'll find plenty of business games in bookshops, schools and colleges, and on computers. This is a simple 'start-up' version of these, encouraging you to imagine being self-employed, and to look at the 'business' element of your idea. So:

- take your best idea, or
- borrow somebody else's, or
- crib from the 'top ten' ideas reported by Shell Livewire (look at its website for more information – see addresses section, page 85): clothes shop, café, landscape gardener, recording studio, graphic designer, hairdresser, car mechanic, computer support, aromatherapist, hand-made toys.

Once you have an idea, decide on a timescale. For this exercise, are you going to look at your business ideas as you are now, or as you might be in, say, two years' time? five years' time?

By setting a date in the future, you can imagine that you already have the education, or the skills, or the money that you currently lack. Then you can see how your idea might pan out in those circumstances. This could help you re-evaluate your plans for the next year or two, depending on how your Virtual Plan goes.

'You need to have a viable business idea. It's very important not to scrimp on the groundwork, such as business plans, because you can see on paper the problems that could occur in the future.' James

The following questions are based on a 'business plan'. You will have to complete a business plan if you approach a bank or other organisation for finance, or if you go to an enterprise agency or similar organisation for advice. Business plans aim to cut through the idealism and ambition within you (only temporarily!) and get you to question things from a business point of view. However dull it seems, it is vital to think this way, as only then can you work out whether your brilliant idea is likely to work, or more likely to put you in debt for years to come.

This is a simplified version – some are horrendously detailed, but you probably don't need that level of detail yet.

'You can do a business plan purely for your own use but you will do it better and be more critical if you're going to present it to someone else: then you question everything from their point of view.' Tim

You can go into self-employment without writing a business plan, if you don't need money or formal advice. Most people setting up in business do tend to want a thorough analysis of their situation and thoughts on paper, though. It is well worth having a go at this, as it pulls in lots more questions. It is really asking the basic, underlying question that this whole section, any agency and any bank is asking: 'Have you thought this out sufficiently?'

Here are the business plan headings.

My business idea is...

'You need to get across at an early stage some sort of visual; for instance, if you want to set up as an accountant, what sort of accountant? What sort of customers? You need to give the reader some sort of understanding of what the core of the business will be about.'
Tim

I am planning this business...

...now/in two years' time, etc.

Personal statement

You need to be clear about your personal goals setting up in self-employment. These might include being independent, being more involved in something that interests you, or losing your job and needing to make a living: whatever it is, think it through and write it down.

Business mission statement

> *'You've got to identify what it is you want to achieve and divide those achievements into short, medium and long term.'* Tim

These are your key business aims. It's worth putting them on paper and referring back to them from time to time; it's very easy to get bogged down with life's minutiae. They might read:

- to provide the best selection of recorded popular music in town;
- to provide this in a comfortable and welcoming setting;
- to build this into the leading music shop in town within three years;
- to make a 30% profit on capital within two years;
- to expand to a second shop in a neighbouring town within five years.

Business name

You need to think out a good name and then display and use it well. It should tell your customers what you do, and sound professional. It helps if it sounds positive and upbeat and sells the business. If it sticks in the mind and has a good twist to it, that's even better. You can get guidance on this from the Companies Registration Office (whether you are a limited company or not), as there are certain rules.

Description of business

This is a description of your products or services. You need to hook people with an image of what you hope to do or produce. Write out exactly what it is that you plan to do.

'You're trying to "up" everyone's confidence in what you're doing. Business plans form part of the confidence-building process when applying for financial support. There's no way that anyone can understand your business idea, however confident you are, unless you have something they can look at that demonstrates how what you say can be put into effect and can work. You must first enthuse them with that document, if that's what they see first.' Tim

Premises

You need to decide where you will be working. This could be from home to start with (though Jim says: *'get yourself somewhere away from home – the house is somewhere to switch off. It's tempting if work is always there, to switch on and do some work. Mentally, you have to have a real break'*) You may begin in an office or unit of some type. Think about planning, building, and health & safety regulations, all the details of the lease and rent, fixtures and fittings, any licences needed, the overall size, location, access and security, and what the whole will cost you.

'Be very wary of premises. Investigate carefully – don't wait until you are committed before carefully costing conversions, repairs etc. Have a survey done. Also look at the length of the lease: you're still responsible for paying the rent even if the business has gone foul.' Tim

You may have little idea, yet, of where you would trade, but see if you can work out the best type of environment and where you would find it.

Personnel

Personnel means the people in the business. It's about you and your education, skills and experience. It includes others you would be setting up with. You need to sell yourself here: give the details, but overall, make sure you explain why you have what is necessary to make a success of this business. This includes your commitment and understanding of what it's like to be in business.

Also add any business training you've had, even a seminar here or there –

it all adds up. Explain why this training will help make your business a success. Remember to think about your and your colleagues' health and other commitments.

The market

Get this section right! Whether for your own use, or to convince someone else, you need to really understand your product/service, its unique selling points, the market you want to launch it in, and why it will succeed. This involves market research (by an agency or by yourself, but properly conceived and conducted) with evidence to show, if necessary. It includes desk and field research: reading around the market, finding trends and statistics, sending questionnaires to potential customers, and so on.

> *'I did a lot of investigating, and went to other playschools. I knew there was the demand for another playgroup. I went and stood outside the local infant school and introduced myself, and handed out flyers I'd had printed. This was before I had set up, to assess the demand. I got a lot of phone calls from that, some people even enrolled their children at that point. So I knew the demand was there.'* Emma

> *'Market research is very important. It's easy to have an idea of what people want, but you're not always right.'* James

You may find it helpful to break it down like this:

- who are your customers?
- methods and results of market research;
- how will you be successful selling to these customers?
- the competition – who/what/where? Why are you better?
- sales and marketing plans, including costs and advertising.

> *'Small businesses can achieve much more at an individual level than wasting money on advertising. With advertising, you've got to be well targeted and have enough money to keep you going until it works.'* Tim

Sales analysis

You need to work out how many/much you plan to sell, how much you need to earn in order to fulfil your plans (to keep eating; to reinvest; and so on), divide one by the other, and that is the cost per item. Will they sell at that price? If not, can you live on less? Can you manufacture more cheaply? Can you make more? You need to note details of:

- materials
- stock
- labour
- heat/light/rent
- other overheads such as admin, travelling costs etc

before you can finalise pricing.

> *'I'm making up a portfolio of photographs, then I can show stuff to people when they enquire. I'm going to work out how much everything costs to make, and write it up.'* Ruth

When working out how many you think you can sell each month, allow for seasonal fluctuations, for getting your name known, for supply problems, etc. This figure goes on the document called your 'cashflow forecast' (see the end of this section). You will need to show how you came to these figures.

Equipment, transport, insurance

Note details of all equipment, from forklifts to letterheads, how much it will cost, whether you'll go for new/second-hand, why you need it at all. Some insurance is required by law (employer's liability, third party motor); other insurance is standard – public liability (to cover against lawsuits for injury etc caused through your business activities); property insurance, against fire and theft, to protect your assets.

There are other insurance policies you can buy into – health insurance, for instance, in case you are unable to work and need immediate medical attention rather than wait for months. Most people starting in business find their margins too tight for all the insurance available; you need to take a view on what is most important at which stage. Research and keep notes of all insurance.

Finance

You can make notes under four main headings:

1. Personal financial profile

This is a financial summary of you, as you are now (or if you are imagining ahead, of how you would be just before you became self-employed), but excluding the income and costs of the business you plan to set up. The bullet points below list the items you need to consider. It includes everything you earn, and all the costs you have to pay. For instance, you might have a temporary job paying the minimum wage, but you live at home and have fairly low outgoings so you're doing well financially. Or you might have to make that same pay stretch to rent and bills and food in a shared house, or to paying a mortgage, or supporting a family.

All these aspects will affect your business plan. For example, they affect how you price your goods or services. If you have low outgoings you don't have to make as much money in your self-employment as somebody who has higher outgoings. So you may be able to price your goods lower and undercut competitors. They also affect how much money you might be able to borrow – if you already have some and are prepared to risk it in setting up a business, then agencies and banks are more likely to lend to you. Or you may not need a loan at all.

You may feel certain of a good income from your self-employment straight away – it may have been promised to you. But even so, you need to know how much it costs you to live for two months, say: one month to set up and start the freelance work, and another to allow for your clients to pay you. Remember too that many clients are slow payers... could you live for a third month, if so?

These are all things you need to think about, and if you have the figures on paper as a personal financial profile, it's easier to look at the true situation and make valid decisions.

Items to consider:

- your estimated annual earnings
- other income you might be able to rely on (family help etc)
- benefits, etc – but remember that unless you start in self-employment under a scheme like New Deal, you will probably no longer receive benefits.

Add these to make your total income for the year.

Then note your likely expenditure:

- Accommodation – rent or mortgage
- Community charge, water rates
- Other bills such as fuel
- Food and other living costs such as clothes, phone bill, insurance, entertainment (including HP on the television etc)
- Vehicle costs
- Family costs, eg presents for family members
- Savings, pension plan

Then add an amount for unexpected expenditure.

Take the total expenditure from the total income. If you have a surplus, you can estimate how much of this you can save to put into a future business.

If you are already spending beyond your means, or only just scraping even, perhaps this is why you want to set up in business – to increase your income. But it means that you have additional pressure to get started, and this pressure can skew your judgement when assessing how viable your self-employment is really going to be. It is not easy to be objective, and when you really want something, it's even easier to slant your thinking, and your estimates. Every adviser would say: slow down, think long and hard, research, research again, and don't start up until you are sure.

Whatever your current situation, look at the expenditure part of the profile: this part remains when you start in self-employment, even though your income may fall (if you give up work to start a business, for instance).

> 'I still work in the trade as a freelance, advising on production, so I've still got cash coming in. But book fairs are limiting on what I can do as a freelance. At the turn of the year I will assess the freelance work again.' Matt.

You need to remain realistic about your outgoings, and how you are going to cover them with your income.

'I started off just covering the rent and my deputy's wage. Luckily my partner supported me. It was a lot of hard work, but I was enjoying it.' Emma

2. Assets

What assets do you have? In other words, what do you own that you could either sell to raise finance, or you could give as security for a loan? This is usually necessary when you borrow money. Unless you can convince the lender that your idea is foolproof and that you will be able to repay the money, the lender will ask you to give something as security. If you own a house, for instance, you may sign an interest in that property to the lender, so that the lender can sell the property and take the money owed if you can't repay the debt.

Many young people setting up in business don't own property. Other assets could be used. If you have some cash, for instance, you might persuade a bank to lend you an equal amount of cash – the bank then knows that you have as much to lose as it does, and has more belief in what you are doing. You may not have any assets at all. In this case there are small grants and loans available through the government and charitable agencies. There is sometimes talk of them 'not being able to give their money away', as their lending criteria can be quite strict – this is not always the case but it's worth investigating. You won't get huge sums this way, though.

'Generally young people won't have any security – so what have you got to make the banks feel confident about you? The only thing is what you write on your business plan, that it is based on sound research and facts and that you yourself can do it, which is where you bring in organisations such as the PYBT. This can show that you are trying to build up a package. Get together little notes {with promises of finance}: you are now in a position to go to the bank – they might lend then, if they're happy with the plan, especially if you've got, say, one thousand pounds of your own: building up layers of confidence. So this way you may get something unsecured.' Tim

3. Operating budget

You need to know before you start how your business will go financially. It's no use learning this from your accountant once a year, several months after the end of your financial year. You need the figures straight away every month, so you can compare them with the projections you make before you start. These projections are your operating budget: you make estimates of everything from fixed costs such as rent, through to variable costs such as materials (which increase or decrease depending how much you sell) and sales figures. All income, and expenses against income, go in here, as realistically as possible. You can then determine whether, if all goes to plan, your business will be successful.

4. Cashflow forecast

You need to find out when you might not have enough cash – before it happens. Lose sight of this, and if you find you cannot pay your supplier, or landlord, that is the end of your business. If you know this in advance, you can plan for it. You can also use your resources more efficiently, and plan for capital expenditure and so on. It is like a real-life version of your operating budget. It takes account of unexpected events: a supplier demands cash-on-delivery, when you had assumed you had 30 days in which to pay, and so on. It includes all money transactions within the business (including capital expenses, which are not in your operating budget). It is a framed painting of your business.

> 'A cashflow forecast doesn't mean anything unless it's backed up by a narrative – an accountant can make any cashflow forecast show something – using an accountant gives it an air of credibility but that's not necessarily good for the person doing it – do your own, as it's the only way you're going to understand it.' Tim

USING YOUR BUSINESS PLAN

This business plan may be just for your benefit, either as an exercise in planning out a possible future venture, or as a real start in business. Or it may be for a bank or other agency. If the latter, you will need to show every working, every piece of evidence (you may be asked for educational or training certificates, or driving licences, or market research results, etc). Even if it is just for you, don't be tempted to be anything other than completely truthful: if you don't get an objective view at this stage, then the whole idea of planning, and its use, goes down the tubes.

'There's no point doing a business plan if you know that what you're putting down is not correct. I have seen people who have been to the banks and the banks have obviously wanted to lend them money, if the paperwork matched the enthusiasm of the individual. Individuals within the banks will on occasion have some feeling of confidence: "we'd like to lend you x but your business plan doesn't look right". It can be disastrous to create a business plan that does not reasonably accurately reflect what you can achieve and how much you may need to borrow and how much you can afford to repay.' Tim

Summary

This business plan is the backbone of your venture into self-employment. Writing it down this way may feel like second-nature, or may feel like a foreign language. If you are going to be self-employed you will need to learn this language at some stage... and it's better to go into that world already speaking the lingo than picking it up as you go along.

'You've really got to know what you're doing with finances. For instance, when I applied for some money from the PYBT, I put down what equipment I wanted, and later realised that I hadn't added VAT! I had to add another 17.5% to the cost of everything. I got the money I asked for, but it meant I bought less equipment.' Emma

There are all sorts of ways of immersing yourself in the world of business plans and financial projections, and they don't have to be dire and boring and squeeze the entrepreneurial spirit out of you (though at times it may feel as though that's happening). Try short courses or enterprise clubs or anything that gives you a gentle introduction. Or get work in a business environment and learn it first-hand. Many successful business people start off with some type of accountancy qualification, for instance, and move in from there.

Whatever happens, hold on to those ideas and ideals, and to the skills portfolio you are building, and keep reviewing where you stand and where you are going.

THE VIRTUAL BUSINESS REVIEW: LOOKING AT HOW YOUR BUSINESS FARED

Sometimes banks and other agencies lend money to people whose businesses then fail. There are also plenty of examples of business people who were turned away from every lending organisation, being told their idea would never work, and then went on to do very well on their own. So, as the banks will tell you, being lent money is not a guarantee of success. Even so, asking yourself whether you would satisfy a bank or agency's criteria is a useful thing to do, as it encourages objectivity.

In the light of your answers to the questions in part 3, Virtually There, (page 50), ask yourself:

Would your business get funding? If not, why not?
 – Wrong personnel?
 – Not enough of your own capital?
 – The cashflow didn't add up?
 – The marketing ideas weren't strong enough?
 – You hadn't had enough advice/support?
 – There were too many market fluctuations you couldn't cope with?
 – The idea wasn't 'selling'?
 – Overall, was it a poor business plan? ...and so on.

You may not know whether your business plan scored high or low: is there someone with business experience you could ask? Explain that it's just an exercise and get their candid view.

Once you have re-evaluated, can you see which areas you have thought through adequately, and those where you need to think further?

Get hold of loads of blank business plans and slot your ideas into them all the time: one for each idea, or one a month, or whatever feels right for you. Get used to the basic principle that entrepreneurial ideas are great, fantastic, they are what our economy depends upon, but they won't work if they're not thought out properly.

It's not only things like the initial investment that have to be right, it's the decisions that are made along the way, the keeping control.

'Maintaining control is a very important aspect of business and the business plan – as soon as you borrow money or take on premises etc, you have lost an element of control.' Tim

So simply starting off well (which you can do with help and advice) isn't enough: you have to get a feel for it all yourself, so that you can continue to monitor and make change where necessary.

Review the business areas that you know less about, using the next section as a starting point for more research. Keep your eyes and ears open for change: business changes, legislation, political change. See how this opens opportunities for new ideas, how it affects businesses, how it might affect yours. Then draw up another business plan and see if it is becoming easier.

Virtual trading

You can extrapolate this Virtual Business Plan, and start virtual trading, if you get the (virtual) backing you need. Work month by month, imagining positive and negative factors. How would you deal with them? How many extra hours would it take? Will the cashflow support it? Are you still sure you want to be self-employed?

HOW DOES THIS SOUND?
(...the bit designed to put you off)

- no paid holidays, and quite possibly no holidays at all;
- very long hours;
- no sick pay;
- no job or financial security;
- having to be constantly aware of changes in the market and supply and government policy etc;
- selling yourself and your wares all the time;
- always being on duty in some sense;
- having to manage other people, often being harsh to people who become your friends;
- being emotionally alone;

- always learning and training and developing your skills;
- always taking decisions;
- knowing that the next recession could finish you off;
- being organised all the time with paperwork and legislative demands.

Many self-employed people are dreamers; this is great, it's what gives us the inspiration to do new things, to believe in ourselves and our abilities. Every business adviser you speak to will say you must also have your feet on the ground and understand the above points – the realities of being self-employed. Knowing this, doing the research and having the skills, both work skills and the get-up-and-go to act on your plans, are the keys to success in self-employment.

> *'You need enthusiasm tempered with a practical awareness and the demonstration that you can actually do it – that phrase "making it happen". You can write it down, but picking up the phone and so on, requires people who will actually act on it, do it.'* Tim

Chapter 5
INFORMATION SECTION

This is an alphabetical listing of many aspects of being self-employed. Each is sketched in very broad outline – you need to get much more information about each of these, and give them serious thought, before committing yourself financially in any way.

Follow these ideas and leads through to the addresses section.

Administration

'I'm exactly the wrong sort of person to set up a business – administration is total anathema to me – my accountant tears his hair out in despair. This matters more and more as Kerb grows – sending invoices out on time, chasing them up. I could hire an administration person but as soon as I have enough money in the pot I hire a creative person.' Jim

It needn't be like this, but many entrepreneurs forget to plan administration into their time and mind-frame: it is easy to get carried away with the core of the idea and setting up the business. It simply won't work if you don't do the admin. Plan for it from the beginning and life will be a great deal easier.

Advisers

There is a wealth of enterprise advice available. The banks will advise you, as will enterprise agencies and, for young people, organisations such as the Prince's Youth Business Trust and Livewire. There may also be local initiatives, networking days and so on. More specifically, there are networking groups for people in certain business areas, where you may be able to ask advice. People will be helpful and encouraging: a healthy market has room for many businesses, especially if yours aims to fill a gap in provision.

'You need to do a lot of groundwork, A lot of people have ideas and rush into it. Ask as many people as you know what they think of your idea. Get input.' Emma

Remember that commercial organisations that give advice need to make money from you in some way; the banks are looking for your business. Their agenda is the same as yours – that you are successful and make money, but they may not offer completely impartial advice the way than agency will.

Banks

Banking is changing but one thing is certain: banks need business accounts in order to make money. They have business units with specialists who can advise on all aspects of your business, from the initial plan right through to problems and, of course, funding. They are in competition for your business, so shop around. The less well-known banks (formerly building societies) are worth approaching for details of their services, and those of their associate organisations if they do not offer business services themselves. Also look at postal banking.

You need a bank for two main things:

- **Finance.** The bank may lend you the money you need to start, and later expand, your business, but you will have to convince them that you know what you are doing.
- **Business banking.** You will not get free banking as you do as a personal customer, and the banks are after your business account.

Get business packs from as many banks as you can – they are full of useful advice.

Book-keeping, accounts

You may do your own book-keeping and accounts, or you may pay someone to do this for you, but what is essential is that you keep every piece of paper that comes into your hands. You will need to complete accounts for your lender (probably the bank) as well as the taxman. You may be able to retrieve information to do this if you keep all your invoices and receipts in one place, but not if you bin them. Better to keep them in as orderly a fashion as possible. It is a chore – very few people enjoy doing their books. It is also a grind on top of running the business itself, and tends to be left to the last minute. It is much, much better if you can get to grips with this as soon as possible. This is not just to help stabilise the workload, but also to help you see where your business is heading.

Have you thought about going on a book-keeping course before you start up? Then you will at least have some idea of how to set up the basic systems you need, even if you don't plan to do the book-keeping yourself. You will also need to learn how to read, and construct, accounts, and talk to advisers and lenders about them. It'll be easier learning this before you are restricted by the inevitable time constraints of running a business.

Business advice – see advisers.

Business expenses

Part of the knack of business is 'balancing' your expenses against your income – if you get it right, the resulting surplus is profit. You need a surplus in order to live on a day-to-day basis. You may also need some to reinvest in the business. This is all a part of your business plan. Remember to keep records of all expenses (see administration, book-keeping).

Business Link

This is a government-funded organisation with branches across the UK. It helps established and growing businesses (not start-up and very small businesses – these are the remit of the Enterprise Agencies). You may need to contact Business Link to find the contacts you need for the Enterprise Agency. It's worth finding out what's going on with your local Business Link anyway.

Business plans

Chapter 4 showed you how to work through a business plan. You can get blank copies from the advisory agencies and the lenders – just ask for their business packs. Some are simple, others more convoluted. Try working through a few (a simple one first) to get into practice.

Business strategy

Do you know what this means? Do you have one? There is a whole industry of business advice, including the teaching you get at school, during a business degree or MBA. Try reading the business pages of the broadsheet newspapers and seeing if you can work out which organisation is doing what at the moment, and what the current business 'fashions' are.

Capital

This is the money you need behind your business, to pay for things like premises and stock, to keep you going until your clients pay you, and so on. You might already have your own capital, or might have to borrow it. You might even be given some, either privately through a relation, say, or from one of the agencies, although this won't be much.

> *'The agency sent some guy round when we were after additional funding. He said "Nah, you won't get any funding, just advice." He said we should get out into the local community more, which was useful. With funding you have to jump through so many hoops, you're better spending that time doing work for your portfolio.'* Jim

Before you start in self-employment you must work out how much capital you need, and how you are going to get it. This is part of the business plan.

Cashflow

If your income arrives too late, then you have cashflow problems. As the previous section of this book described, there's no point invoicing huge sums of money through your fantastic new business if people or organisations take months to pay, and you don't have the cash behind you. Maybe then you can't meet the rent on your premises, say, and get thrown out. A lot of the money lent by banks is to get businesses through these cashflow crises. It's vital to plan for cashflow fluctuations, and know where the money is coming from. Equally, there will be times when you have surplus cash and want to invest it. Drawing up cashflow forecasts helps predict all this.

Chambers of Commerce

These are local organisations of people in business, who get together for all sorts of reasons. They offer support and training to new businesses, and are a great way into networking with people in a similar line, and potential suppliers and customers.

Collectives

Some people choose to set up organisations called collectives, where every member has equal ownership of the organisation, equal income, and an equal say in the running of the business. More information from The Industrial Common Ownership Movement (ICOM) – see contacts in Chapter 6

Company director

There are different ways of structuring your business, to help save tax, to decrease liability, and so on. One of these is to set up a limited company, with yourself as one of the directors. In some areas of self-employment everyone does this. In others, nobody does. In some, people organise their employment structure in a variety of ways. Strictly speaking, when you are working as a company director you are not self-employed, but employed by the shareholders. If, however, you are the only shareholder (ie you own the company) it's fair to say that you are still self-employed. (See also 'Sole trader', and 'Partnership').

Contractor

This has two meanings. Traditionally it means somebody (or an organisation) who agrees to manage a project, perhaps in the building trade. This person then subcontracts, or farms out, individual pieces of work to specialists such as carpenters or electricians. More recently, 'contractors' has also come to mean highly skilled people in the computing industry who, instead of working as employees for one organisation, work on short-term contracts of perhaps three months to two years. They may then move on to another organisation. These people are effectively self-employed, though they do set up limited companies to organise the tax side of their work.

Cooperatives

Cooperatives are similar to collectives, though they can be run on a much larger scale. This is possible as the members do not all take part in the decision-making processes. Also, members may be paid according to their seniority. The profit all goes to the members (workers, usually) of the cooperative, rather than external owners or shareholders.

Costing & pricing

When you provide a service or product you need to price it right: it has to be saleable (which usually means not too expensive) and also bring in enough income to cover your overheads and living expenses and justify running the business. Knowing how to price appropriately involves close analysis of the market (market research) and the cost to you of producing the goods or services. It is a complex area; for instance, some goods may actually sell better when priced higher, if customers are convinced that the product or service is worth the money and are looking for something up-market.

Customs & Excise

This is the government agency that runs the tax called VAT (see below). It also administers duty on alcohol, gaming licences, and imports and exports. You need to get in touch with HM Customs & Excise when starting in self-employment, to see how VAT affects what you do, and possibly with regard to other issues too.

Department of Trade & Industry

This is a government department that aims *'to increase UK competitiveness and scientific excellence in order to generate higher levels of sustainable growth and productivity in a modern economy'* (DTI website). It has many different divisions and units, including those focusing on small businesses. Look up the DTI website for an overview of the areas it covers.

Employment issues

Perhaps you will only employ yourself, or you may immediately, or over time, employ other people. Staffing a business is thought by many to be one of the great headaches: finding the right people, offering competitive pay, managing them once they work for you, training them, retaining them, keeping them busy and effective even in slack periods, sorting out and paying their tax and National Insurance, and generally looking after them and keeping them happy. No wonder so many employers opt for short-term contracts!
Yet its staff make an organisation, and the fashion for delayering and downsizing (pushing out whole layers of people, and increasing the productivity of those left, while using freelance or contract labour where necessary) is now reversing.

Employers see how important it is to have a constant and motivated workforce. In a small business, having the right people on board is critical. You need to consider how your staffing needs might change, and what you would do about it if they did. There are plenty of good books on human resources management, as well as sections of the general books on running small businesses.

Enterprise Agencies

> *'The Enterprise Agency was definitely trying to put you off: so-and-so failed, etc. I went on a two-day Enterprise Agency course on business and the arts. It was for people who planned to set up in business in the next three months. It was very interesting.'* Ruth

These are the local offices that advise people starting up in business, as well as people running small businesses (people running larger businesses go to Business Link). Find details of yours in the phone book under 'Enterprise' or via your TEC/LEC or Business Link offices.

Enterprise Councils – see TECs.

Entrepreneurs

These are people who start up a business or enterprise, with the aim of making money from it (and the possibility of loss, if it doesn't work out). In other words, they are people who take business risks. If you are going into self-employment, you become an entrepreneur.

Franchising

This is described on page 13. It means making a payment for the use of a ready-made business idea along with its name, marketing, management expertise and other backup, such as advertising, supplies and equipment. Contact the British Franchise Association (BFA) for more information.

Freelance

This describes people who sell their skills, rather than use their skills to make something and sell that. Freelances tend to work in areas such as design, writing, consultancy and so on.

Funding

> *'You shouldn't spend any money initially – look for free support until you've worked it all out, identified a market and know that your idea has some sense.'* Tim

Yet at some point, most people going into self-employment need to borrow money.

> *'The next step was finance, I went to the PYBT. You've got to have some money to survive.'* Emma

Here are places to try:

- your local Enterprise Agency.
- organisations such as the Princes Youth Business Trust and Livewire.
- your New Deal personal adviser.
- the high street banks.

If you start at the Enterprise Agency, advisers can tell you about the best place for your particular needs. Don't go to unknown private individuals or small organisations. If you borrow privately from someone you know, or someone who is recommended to you by someone you trust, make sure the details are agreed and put in writing. There are various types of business loans and schemes available, such as Flexible Business Loans for sums of £25,001–£250,000, and the Loan Guarantee Scheme operated by the government, the government providing the security.

Health & Safety

There are regulations governing the health and safety of everybody at work – even just you, working for yourself. Once you start employing other people, handling foodstuffs or dangerous substances, or working with machinery, the regulations get more complex. It is vital that you know what you have to do to protect yourself and others in the workplace. (Contact the Health & Safety Executive.)

Help!

You will need business advice, and possibly continuing help with a mentor. You may get this informally through your own contacts, but there is plenty of good advice available free or at a subsidised rate. It's worth at least finding out about. For free business advice, look at the list of organisations under 'Funding'; also browse on the Internet – see the list of useful websites.

Ideas

Try keeping a log of your ideas, and other interesting ideas you have noticed around you, however daft. Try them on family and friends. Sometimes the peculiar ones do actually work – thrash them out with people who might become your customers – do they have a need that your service or product might fulfil? Is there a special angle to your idea, a unique selling point (USP)? It could take years for the right idea to come, or years for the market to be ready for your brilliant idea. If you note and review them all, you remain a step ahead of potential competition.

Information

You will have a constant need for up-to-date information on all business issues, as well as what is happening in your local and trading communities, nationally, and globally. Your local reference library is a good place to keep up-to-date: enlist the help of a librarian and track down business journals and directories. The Internet is a wonder: everything is there at the touch of a button, and it is kept updated. You do need access to this, certainly when starting up, and hopefully as a tool for continually updating your knowledge. Chapter 6 gives a few websites to start with. Radio, TV and the press are also important for watching trends and spotting emerging markets. Professional bodies and trade organisations in your field are also worth contacting. Follow up leads as you come across them in your research trail.

For industry-specific information, keep in touch with groups of people working locally in the same markets, and read the technical press in your subject areas.

Inland Revenue

'You've got to keep receipts for everything. So many people go in hard against the tax man – if you don't keep receipts the IR won't give any leverage at all.' Jim

You have to pay tax on your earnings, whether you are employed or self-employed. The system varies according to the structure of work you do. You also have to pay tax on behalf of your employees, which means docking it from their wages and paying it to the Inland Revenue at appropriate times. You must understand the tax system and the type of tax you will be paying, and register with them as soon as you become self-employed. There are plenty of free Inland Revenue leaflets, as well as books on running a small business, which detail the tax system. National Insurance contributions are now also collected by the Inland Revenue.

Instant Muscle

> *'IM's prime objective is to focus and support unemployed people towards being in control of their own futures, whether that entails starting up a small business, or fostering the impetus and confidence needed to find a job. If you are aged between 18 and 60 we can offer you confidential and friendly advice and training on a one to one basis to help you.'* Instant Muscle website

Insurance

See page 55. You should shop around for good rates – ask advisers at the Enterprise Agency and elsewhere. You will find differences in premiums with different insurance companies, but you will also find differences in the cover you get. While some types of insurance is required by law and other types are optional, it is worth considering what you would do if there was a fire in your premises, for instance, and you had no insurance cover. It is worth budgeting for a reasonable level of insurance.

Interests

Sometimes people have interests or hobbies that become their work. If you had a passion for photography, for instance, you might want a career in photography. While this often works out, it is worth considering whether, for example as a creative photographer, you would want to be sent on commercial photographic assignments. There are few jobs at the top of any profession, and some people feel they lose their original interest by working in the mundane side of the industry.

Information and communications technology (ICT)

You'll need ICT skills, as well as appropriate equipment and software, if you are self-employed. You should already be gaining ICT skills within education, but may find there are other applications you need once you are trading. These might be for simple functions, like labelling envelopes, or more complex ones, such as payroll or control systems. Once you are self-employed it may be harder to find time to go to college and train.

Some training consultants will come to your offices and spend concentrated training time with you, but this is expensive. More and more organisations, such as secondary schools, make use of their ICT facilities to train members of the public 'out of hours'. Try the Learning Direct phone information service for details of local courses and training opportunities.

You need to budget for the ICT hardware and software necessary for your business. Research the systems used by your competitors. Think ahead to possible expansion needs. Talk it through with someone knowledgeable in both your area of work and business, and in ICT, before making major buying decisions.

Legislation

There is an enormous bank of legislation covering all aspects of self-employment, from employment and health & safety laws through to international trading requirements, and so on.

> *'There's so much legislation running a company that you can be contravening all these regulations you don't know about. It's a minefield.'* Jim

Yet you need to know about the legislation to adhere to it; penalties for non-compliance can be severe, ignorance being no defence.

But the government agencies make it as easy as possible for non-specialists to understand what they need to do. All the agencies (such as the Inland Revenue) have leaflets written in (relatively) plain English. These take time to read and digest, but it is spelled out as simply as possible. Contact all relevant agencies (advisers at the various agencies will give you a list) and work out in advance what you need to do. If you wait until you have started trading you may find you are already contravening legislation. You may even find that your premises are too small or unsuitable for the purpose you have just signed the lease for! Find out early.

Livewire

'Shell Livewire is one of our most ambitious community sponsorships. It aims to support young entrepreneurs who want to set up their own business. We do this by providing free help, advice, literature and expertise to 16–30 year olds. Thousands of young people want to make this giant leap each year, but many start off with unrealistic expectations of what's involved. Shell Livewire gives these young people a better chance of success. We run Shell Livewire in partnership with local Enterprise Agencies, the Prince's Youth Business Trust and Training and Enterprise Councils (TECs), who share resources to provide an outstanding service for young entrepreneurs. More than 16,000 young people get in touch with us each year.' Livewire website

Loans – see funding.

Management

This is a general term used in all sorts of situations – you will manage your finances, your orders, your staff, your everything. This might entail solely bookwork, or hands-on specialist work through the night at your premises, or person-to-person work. You also manage your business as a whole. All of these involve reviewing the situation and the strategies you have in place, seeing how they match up, and taking action to ensure the best result, whatever that is projected to be.

You can spend years learning to 'manage', by correspondence through to HND, degree and MBA courses, or it can be intuitive, with information and procedures gleaned as you go. Most people pull in a mix of these. There are always new trends in management theory, and scores of books and magazines written on the subject.

Marketing

This is the whole 'customer' side of being self-employed, right from the planning stage, when you first start to think about who your customers might be, through market research and sales strategy to closing the sale.

It's easy to think that marketing just falls into place, but getting it wrong means no customers, which means no business.

Market research

This means looking at the market (your customers and potential customers) and working out what they are currently buying, what they want to buy and whether they would buy what you plan to sell. It's easy to slant market research to suit your preconceptions, which can be disastrous. This is one of the reasons for independent market research organisations, which you can commission to look objectively at the market for you. Although this might be too expensive and elaborate, you certainly need to read, talk and structure your market research to be as comprehensive and objective as possible.

Mentors

These are experienced people who take you 'under their wing' and give you the benefit of their wisdom over a period of time. A relation or family friend might already act as your mentor. There are mentoring schemes run through organisations such as the Prince's Youth Business Trust. An appropriate experienced person will meet with you periodically, and will review your business plan and your progress. They will make suggestions but not tell you what to do: the decisions are still yours.

National Insurance

Everyone needs to pay National Insurance (NI), or gain exemption from it if they're not earning. The rates vary according to how much you, or your business, earn. It used to be run by the Contributions Agency within the DSS, but this has now merged with the Inland Revenue. Look in your phone book for your local office for details of the NI system. In the same way as paying income tax for employees, you also need to pay NI on their behalf.

New technology

There is no doubt that information and communications technologies are the basis of how the business world gets its work done. This is true now, and will become more so as time goes on. If you don't understand the technologies it will be a lot harder out there. Even if IT (or ICT) is, to you, only a means to an end, still make sure you keep up-to-date with developments, both generally and in your specific area.

Overseas business

This could be crucial or irrelevant to your self-employment idea at the moment. It is quite likely, though, that you will come across opportunities to sell or buy overseas in the future, and more so as the economy continues to become more global. Obvious countries for trade are those within the EU but almost any country is accessible to UK business, and many offer excellent new markets. Find out about possibilities from organisations such as the Institute of Export.

Partnership

This is when you are in business with one or more other people (usually 2–20 people), but haven't formed a limited company. A partnership agreement needs to be drawn up to cover who does what, who contributed what, who gets what, and how it would be wound up should the partnership end.

Personal adjustments

How do you come across to other people? How do you approach your work? It's possible that you might need to change yourself in some way in order to impress other people in whatever line you are thinking of going into. Do you see this as personal development, or as a necessary evil? Which might be the best approach, for you, in the long term?

Also, as being self-employed is ultimately about carrying the responsibility yourself, are you going to complain and blame everyone else whenever things go wrong? Are you going to rant and rave at the bank for not giving you that last-minute loan, when really you should have anticipated the need for the cash, and sorted it out earlier? You, and your family and friends, will need to make adjustments: all change comes easier when they are anticipated and planned for.

Planning

It's all about planning. Planning includes your original Great Idea and follows through to a constant revision of where you are, where you are going, what else is happening, and a willingness to change your original plans as necessary. Most people plan in their heads as well as on paper. You'll need to put it all on paper at some stage: the business plan, your financial records, and so on. You may also find it useful to keep a more personal record of your ideas (as discussed above) and how you might develop these now or in the future.

Premises

You need somewhere to be self-employed. It could be your living room, someone else's house or garden, leased premises, or somewhere completely different. Clearly, if you work from home and there is no additional cost to you, it will be easier, financially, to start up. People profiled in this book found provincial town-centre offices housing two to four workers for as little as £20–30 a week. They moved from home-working because the stresses of living and working in the same place were too onerous.

If you are manufacturing, or retailing, or handling certain types of materials, planning permission becomes a more important issue: many people work from home without a 'change of use' permission, and only have the occasional visitor, but you can't do this if your activity is going to affect the neighbours or endanger your clients. Talk to planning officers, estate agents and others in your line of business. Keep an eye on the level of leaseholds and rents payable and on what is happening in the commercial premises market. Think about insurance. Tie all this in to your plans.

Present circumstances profile

See the Virtually There section for details of this (page 56). Effectively, it means detailing all your financial outgoings and commitments and working out how much you need to earn from your self-employment in order to survive financially. If it doesn't look healthy, there are often ways of tightening belts to bring the total down, but there's no point doing it unless you are realistic. Looking at your plans in this way can often help you see that an idea could be viable, or plainly isn't.

Prince's Youth Business Trust

Since 1986, the Prince's Trust has helped over 40,000 young people to start their own business, providing loans, bursaries, ongoing advice, business support and marketing opportunities. To qualify for support you must be: aged 18–30; unemployed or 'underemployed' (not fulfilling your full potential); and unable to raise funding elsewhere. You must also have a business idea and the enthusiasm and commitment to make it work. The Prince's Youth Business Trust has over 50 offices around the country. (See the PYBT website.)

Private limited company

This is a 'format' for trading, rather than being a sole trader or partnership. A limited company is separate from its owners, so its owners are not liable for its debts. The company must be properly registered and submit statutory financial statements. Most new business people start trading as sole traders or partnerships.

Profit & loss account

This is a projection of the profit or loss the business thinks it will achieve, or has achieved. It forms part of the accounts.

Risk

Becoming self-employed is risky. Nobody guarantees anything, and your financial survival is entirely in your own hands. You could lose your business, your livelihood, even your home if a loan is secured on it. This could be through a change in circumstance beyond your control (though see 'Personal adjustments' – you cannot go round blaming other people, or life becomes one long negative tirade). Entrepreneurs like independence, and can live with that risk. Remember that no one has any guarantees of security – people with jobs could lose them any time, whatever their employers tell them. It may 'feel' more secure in a job but that's the way ostriches feel when they put their heads in the sand.

Security (on a loan etc)

If you borrow money, the lender will need to be convinced that you can pay it back. The best way of convincing them is to put up an asset as security: you may sign your house over to them, so that they can have the house if you cannot pay back the loan because your business has failed. You may be able to get some funding without security (see Chapter 4). Some entrepreneurs will not risk their homes in their business, and it is certainly easier now to become self-employed without nearly as much capital; some businesses operate from spare rooms and through the Internet, say, and cost relatively little to set up.

As one experienced entrepreneur puts it: *'I won't risk my family home. It's so easy to go wrong. If I can't get someone else to put the money up, then I'm not selling the idea well enough, or it's not a good enough idea.'* This is easier in certain sectors, such as the new technologies where venture capital organisations are actively looking for projects to invest in. If you are looking at a relatively old-fashioned idea, such as setting up in retail, then the same interest probably won't be there. In this situation, you need to asses the risk very carefully.

Selling

If you can't sell, it won't work.

'I think I'm a natural born salesman.' Christos

Even if you are of the 'natural salesperson' type, you will do it better with some training. This is a relatively easy skill to get experience in, as many organisations constantly recruit and train salespeople (often part-time) and expect a large turnover of staff. You could try commission-only selling: it will harden you up, if nothing else. If you do, make sure you find out about the company's training scheme, and that it will invest in you in that way.

We tend to think that salespeople are pushy and irritating. It needn't be like that: good salespeople listen to what their clients want and explain how their service or product can deliver this. Customers want to be asked to buy. They need what you offer. You must get over the reluctance to ask anything of anyone, or you won't get anywhere in business.

> *'I'm a born exhibitionist. I have a dangerous amount of confidence – you need that to go pitching to people. If you were a really shy person you'd be terrified talking to a room of 12 people.'* Jim

But shy people can overcome, and even enjoy, this aspect of the work. It's certainly easier when it's your own product and service you are selling, and you believe in it.

Skills

Work is about skills. Your whole working life is about learning and developing skills. These are what you sell, directly to an employer or indirectly to a customer. See the section on skills, on page 28.

Sole trader

This is the most common form of business ownership. People have the freedom to choose how to do things and the business is relatively simple to manage. However, there is unlimited liability, meaning that you are personally liable for any business debts.

Standards

You have your own standards, and standards will be imposed on you – by legislation, by having to compete, by the demands of your customers. Think about the standard of the service or product you are planning. Do you know the legal requirements? Are you prepared to take these seriously (they are closely monitored in every area, and inspectors will put you out of business if you fail to comply)? Do you know what your competitors are doing? Perhaps your business is based on providing the same type of thing but at a different standard, higher or lower, to reach a different market. Have you thought about the standard of work you need to put into your business in order to satisfy your personal expectations?

Strategy

You need a business strategy. It may be scribbled on the back of an envelope but you still need to know what you are doing. Do you? There are lots of different business strategies, and hundreds of books and articles written about them. Even if you don't want to look in that much depth right now, think about how you would progress your business and what sort of things you would do to reach your final aims.

Tax

The main tax people pay is income tax, payable on all types of earnings as well as income such as bank interest. Employers pay income tax for their staff, so when you have a job you don't have that responsibility, but once you are self-employed you are responsible for paying your own tax (as well as NI, and for getting the VAT right) and so you need accurate records of all your income and expenditure. The Inland Revenue is the organisation that administers income tax.

People generally try to pay as little tax as possible. Doing this legally is called avoidance, and illegally is called evasion. Tax avoidance schemes keep accountants in fees, and can save you a lot of money, but equally, there may be nothing special that can be done in your circumstances to lessen your tax bill. If you do go to an accountant about your tax, get a recommendation first. The best way to keep your tax low is to keep records of all your business expenses, as most of these can be offset against income for tax purposes. (See also VAT.)

Trade and professional associations

These are formed by members with businesses of specific types, to help and support each other through a variety of activities and publications, etc. Contact the trade association in your specialist area to see how they can help.

Training and Enterprise Councils, and Local Enterprise Companies in Scotland (TECs and LECs)

'Training and Enterprise Councils will assist the United Kingdom to become the most prosperous society in the European Community by placing education, training and enterprise in the broader context of economic and industrial development.' TEC website

TECs work with enterprise and entrepreneurs at all levels, as well as administering schemes like modern apprenticeships and other training initiatives for young people. Contact your local TEC/LEC to see how they can help you.

Unique selling point

Every product or service has one – it's what makes yours better than everyone else's. It is used in sales, to convince customers to buy your products or services. When planning your self-employment, look at your ideas and think what your USPs will be: perhaps you can supply something of the same quality but more cheaply, or faster, or offer a guarantee. Perhaps your service is unique, or the only one in the UK. Whatever it is, use this concept to consider whether what you plan to make or provide is really going to find a niche in the marketplace.

VAT

This is value added tax, which is the tax that businesses charge when they supply their goods and services. Small businesses (with a turnover of less than around £50,000) do not register for VAT, and so do not charge their customers VAT. They do have to pay VAT on goods or services they buy in, though. Once registered, these 'input' and 'output' taxes are offset against each other. If your outputs (that is the tax you charge when you supply goods or services) is greater than your inputs then you pay the difference to Customs and Excise. If it is less, then they pay you the difference. Some goods and services are exempt from VAT, others are charged at a nil rate, or a rate less than the current full 17.5%. You need to find out about VAT before you become self-employed.

Year in Industry

This offers students who are expecting good A-level results, and who are interested in engineering, science, business or computing, the chance to spend a paid year in industry before starting their degree course. These placements even to develop skills and increase employability. There are around 500 places available each year. See the Year in Industry website for more information.

Chapter 6
WHERE TO FIND OUT MORE

READING

There are plenty of general and specific books available on starting and running a small business. Look in your school/college and public libraries, and in bookshops.

There are also lots of free leaflets giving summaries and overviews in specific areas. For instance, the Inland Revenue will send you a booklet outlining the requirements for people setting up in business regarding tax, National Insurance and VAT. When researching, and certainly before making detailed plans, phone around and get as many of these as possible.

WEBSITES

Once you get into a good web trail you won't know where to stop... discover all the information you could ever want on any business topic, where to get more information and help, find games and quizzes. It goes on and on. Here are a few starting points:

www.inreach.com/sbdc/book
(US site, so some details and regulations will be different from the UK – still a good site to browse)

www.shell-livewire.org

business.dis.strath.ac.uk SME owner/manager

www.bbc.co.uk/education/blood

www.economist.com

www.bbc.co.uk/education/make

http://bized.ac.uk

www.u-net.com/bureau/net/home.htm

www.bbc.co.uk/education/lzone

www.bbc.co.uk/education/archive.shtml

USEFUL CONTACTS

British Franchise Association
Thames View
Norton Road
Henley on Thames
Oxon RG9 1HG
Tel: 01491 578049
www.british-franchise.org.uk

Contributions Agency
Look in the phone book for your local office.
(NI now collected through Inland Revenue)
www.dss.gov.uk/ca/

Department of Trade & Industry
1 Victoria Street
London SW1H 0ET
Tel: 0171 215 5000
www2.dti.gov.uk and www.dti.gov.uk

Employers' Helpline
For information on PAYE, National Insurance, VAT etc.
Tel: 0345 143143

HM Customs and Excise
Look in your local phone book under 'Customs and Excise'.
www.open.gov.uk/customs/c&ehome/htm

Health & Safety Executive
Magdalen House
Stanley Precinct
Bootle
Merseyside L20 3QZ
Tel: 0151 951 400
Health & Safety homepage: www.rmarlowe.freeserve.co.uk

ICOM: Industrial Common Ownership Movement
Vassalli House
20 Central Road
Leeds LS1 6DE
Tel: 0113 246 1738
(no website at present)

Inland Revenue
Look in your phone book for your local office
www.open.gov.uk/inrev/irhome.htm

Instant Muscle
Springside House
84 North End Road
London W14 9ES
Tel: 0171 603 2604
www.cf.ac.uk/ccin/main

Institute of Export
Export House
64 Clifton Street
London EC2A 4HB
Tel: 0171 247 9812
Fax: 0171 377 5343
www.export.org.uk
e-mail: institute@export.org.uk

Learning Direct
A national freephone number to research local training opportunities.
Freefone: 0800 100900

Livewire
Hawthorn House
Firth Banks
Newcastle upon Tyne NE1 3SG
Tel: 0191 261 5584
www.shell-livewire.org

Prince's Youth Business Trust
18 Park Square East
London NW1 4LH
Tel: 0171 543 1234
More info: 0800 842842
www.princes-trust.org.uk

Tomorrow's People
Suite 4, Thrift House
13–15 Wallington Place
Hastings
East Sussex TN34 1NY
Tel: 01424 718491
(no website at present)

Training and Enterprise Councils, and Local Enterprise Companies in Scotland (TECs and LECs)
These may be named under the county name rather than by 'TEC' or 'LEC' in the phone book. Try the website to find your local TEC/LEC, or look under 'Business Link' in the phone book.
www.tec.co.uk

The Year in Industry
Simon Building
University of Manchester
Oxford Road
Manchester M13 9PL
Tel: 0161 275 4396
www.eyecue.co.uk/eyecue/yini/

UCAS
Rosehill
New Barn Lane
Jessop Avenue
Cheltenham
Glos GL52 3LZ
Tel: 01242 222444